Your Faith Is Your Fortune

Your Unlimited Power

A Metaphysical Compilation

Compiled and Edited

by

David Allen

2018

Copyright © 2018 by Shanon Allen / David Allen

All rights reserved. No part of this publication may be reproduced, distributed, or transmitted in any form or by any means, including photocopying, recording, or other electronic or mechanical methods, without the prior written permission of the publisher, except in the case of brief quotations embodied in critical reviews and certain other noncommercial uses permitted by copyright law.
Printed in the United States of America (1)

First Printing, April 2018

ISBN: 978-0-9995435-3-5

Visit Us At **NevilleGoddardBooks.com** for a complete listing of all our books and **1000's of Free Books to Read online and download.**

Published
by
Shanon Allen
Copyright © 2018

Disclaimer: All books that have been used in the creation of Your Faith Is Your Fortune: Your Unlimited Power are either in the public domain because of being published prior to 1923 or they were published between 1923 and 1978 and the copyright was never renewed. If you feel we are in error please contact us with the correct information. Should we be in error, we apologize as it is not our intent to violate any copyright laws.

Foreword

This book is an attempt to capture the essence of Faith. what it is and what it means to us. There are definitions, interpretations, and varying uses and applications for practical everyday use, including how it applies to the Law of Attraction. It is intended to enlighten and illumine the conscious mind of the reader that there is power in this gift (Faith) that we all possess and it is unlimited in use. As the words on these pages begin to interact with your mind, we believe you will be amazed how much more there is to Faith than you previously were aware of. Having a better understanding of Faith, when applied to your everyday life, will prove to be a power and a gift that can and will transform your life much to your own amazement.

As with any metaphysical book I would recommend to periodically re-read Your Faith Is Your Fortune: Your Unlimited Power, every so often, as there is a tendency, especially with metaphysical books, to have the words penetrate our subconscious minds and with the passage of time, our own spiritual growth and upon reflection and contemplation, give us a new understanding that we did not previously possess on the first reading. Allow Your Faith Is Your Fortune: Your Unlimited Power to open up new doors in your life.

This book was previously published under the name The Power and The Law of Faith.

David Allen

Acknowledgments

Your Faith Is Your Fortune: Your Unlimited Power is a compilation of the metaphysical interpretations of Faith and how we can apply it in our life, by the following 26 authors:

James Allen
William Walker Atkinson
Genevieve Behrend
Venice J. Bloodworth
Thomas Parker Boyd
Uriel Buchanan
W. J. Colville
Malinda Elliott Cramer
Florence Gloria Crawford
Theron Q. Dumont
Warren Felt Evans
Orison Swett Marden
Charles Fillmore
Henry Wilder Foote
Neville Goddard
Charles T. Gorham
Fenwicke L. Holmes
William Ralph Inge
Christian D. Larson
Samuel McComb
Charles Edgar Prather
Robert A. Russell
Florence Scovel Shinn
Ralph Waldo Trine
Frances Larimer Warner
Wallace Wattles

The sum total of our life is that upon which we have concentrated. If poverty or opulence, if success or failure, if prosperity or want has occupied our minds, if we have focused our attention upon one of these, that is just what we shall see incorporated in our life. What you have, my friend, what you have surrounded yourself with, is a reproduction of your thought, your faith, your belief in your efforts; is what you have been conscious of. Our thoughts, our faith, our beliefs, our efforts, all materialize, and are objectified about us. Our words become flesh and live with us; our thoughts, our emotions, become flesh and live with us; they become our environment and surround us.

It was intended that we should have an abundance of the good things of the universe. None of them are withheld from us except by our poverty-stricken mental attitude. There is no more possible lack for a human being of all that the heart can wish for than there is lack of water or food supply for the fish in the great ocean. The fish swims in the ocean of supply, as we swim in the great cosmic ocean of supply that is all around us. All we have to do is to open our minds, our faith, our confidence, to its reality, and use our intelligent effort to get all the good there is in it, — that is everything we need and desire.

A great many of those who fail in life, or who attain only mediocre positions, keep themselves back by self-depreciation, by a lack of faith in their own powers, the suggestion of their own inferiority. Nothing is more detrimental to success than this sort of mental attitude. It would take the stamina out of a Napoleon. The instant you acknowledge that you are incapable of doing the thing you attempt to do, or that anything can permanently block the way to the goal of your ambition, you set up a barrier to your success that no amount of hard work can remove. He can who thinks he can, holds true in every situation of life.

Hold the thought that you are one with what you want, that you are in tune with it, so as to attract it; keep your mind vigorously concentrated upon it; never doubt your ability to get what you are after, and you will tend to get it. Poverty is often a mental disease. If you are suffering from it, if you are a victim of it, you will be surprised to see how quickly your condition will improve when you change your mental attitude, and, instead of holding that miserable, shriveled, limited poverty image, turn about and face towards abundance and plenty, towards freedom and happiness. Success comes through a perfectly scientific mental process. The man who becomes prosperous believes that he is going to be prosperous. He has faith in his ability to make money. He does not start out with his mind filled with doubts and fears, and all the time talk poverty and think poverty, walk like a pauper and dress like a pauper. He turns his face towards the thing he is trying for and is determined to get, and will not admit its opposite picture in his mind.

A new world dawns for us every morning. Everything in it is fresh and unknown. To the hopeful and daring soul, each day is a thrilling adventure. What it will bring, he does not know. That it will be good, he can but believe. This belief is his Faith. We all live by Faith for we are always on the borderland of the future. Each act is an act of Faith . . a feeling beforehand that the thing we are doing will bring results of some sort and usually of the kind that we expect. And the deeper this feeling is, the more certain are the results.

Faith is not mere belief; neither is it a doctrine about anything that was, is, or is to be. Faith and belief have nothing in common; they are as different as darkness and light. Belief is human; Faith is more than human; belief knows nothing; Faith knows everything. The true Faith is a spiritual state of mind; a state of mind that is very deep, very high, and beautiful beyond description. It is a State of mind that knows; and it knows, because to be in Faith is to be upon the mountaintop of intelligence, wisdom and illumination.

You are by the attitude of thought you hold always drawing to you corresponding conditions which are beneficial or injurious. There is a mental state which, if permanently held to, will draw to you all that is desirable. If you are always calm and determined and have an unwavering purpose, you will attract to you from the invisible domain the things you silently demand. But if you lack Faith and are haunted by fear and uncertainty, you will drive happiness from you and will attract misfortune and failure.

Faith always brings us into harmony with the inner, finer essence of things; hence its enormous power. Faith opens the door to the great unknown, and proves that the great unknown is simply an extension . . an endless extension, of that which is known.

"If you desire Faith," **says Browning,** "then you've Faith enough." There is a profound truth here, for it is the desires that reveal the real as distinguished from the apparent trend of the inner life, and if the desire be strong enough the end will be achieved. There is nothing more true to experience than this: that if we really wish for Faith we will get Faith, and if we do not get it, it is because we do not really wish it.

Remember to begin the solution of your problem . . the fulfillment of your need . . in the true place: "In the beginning . . God (consciousness)." Spirit, the Father, is the source and substance of every needful thing. Therefore, the first step in demonstration is to recognize that whatever you desire, its beginning, or source, is God (consciousness), and you must go to the Father for it, knowing for a certainty that if you ask for bread you will not receive a stone, but will receive exactly that for which you ask.

Faith not only gives superiority to the intellect, but elevates the mind to a higher and higher state of comprehension, so that an ever-increasing world of thought and life is incorporated in the scope of mentality. This gives added power and quality to every talent, and opens consciousness to the limitless source of everything that mind may require.

The term blind Faith is an instinctive trust in a power higher than ourselves. Because blind Faith does not understand the principles of Being, it is liable to discouragement and disappointment.

Neville on Manifesting your Desires

Stop asking yourself whether you are worthy or unworthy to receive that which you desire. You, as man, did not create the desire. Your desires are ever fashioned within you because of what you now claim yourself to be. When a man is hungry, (without thinking) he automatically desires food. When imprisoned, he automatically desires freedom and so forth. Your desires contain within themselves the plan of self-expression. So leave all judgments out of the picture and rise in consciousness to the level of your desire and make yourself one with it by claiming it to be so now. For: "My grace is sufficient for thee. My strength is made perfect in weakness." Have Faith in this unseen claim until the conviction is born within you that it is so. Your confidence in this claim will pay great rewards. Just a little while and he, the thing desired, will come. But without Faith it is impossible to realize anything. Through Faith the worlds were framed because — "Faith is the substance of the thing hoped for — the evidence of the thing not yet seen." Don't be anxious or concerned as to results. They will follow just as surely as day follows night. Look upon your desires — all of them — as the spoken words of God (consciousness), and every word or desire a promise. The reason most of us fail to realize our desires is because we are constantly conditioning them. Do not condition your desire. Just accept it as it comes to you. Give thanks for it to the point that you are grateful for having already received it – then go about your way in peace. Such acceptance of your desire is like dropping seed — fertile seed — into prepared soil. For when you can drop the thing desired in consciousness, confident that it shall appear, you have done all that is expected to you. But, to be worried or concerned about the HOW of your desire maturing is to hold these fertile seeds in a mental grasp, and, therefore, never to have dropped them in the soil of confidence.

The most important thing in Faith is its polarity. If your Faith is positive, your thoughts will be positive, your words will be positive, and you will attract the best of everything. If your Faith is negative, your thoughts will be negative, your words will be negative and you will attract the worst of everything. The polarity of your Faith determines the results. If you have been living, thinking, acting, speaking on the negative side of life, the polarity of your Faith needs changing.

We all realize that unlimited possibilities are latent in the great within; and we are all in search of the best and most thorough methods through which these possibilities may be developed; but it has been discovered that the within is unfolded only through the expansion of consciousness; how to expand consciousness, therefore, becomes one of the greatest problems in the life of man. It is solved, however, through Faith; Faith expands consciousness; in fact, it is only through Faith that consciousness may be expanded. This is a fact of extreme importance, a fact that every metaphysician and psychologist should note with care, and act accordingly. The absence of real Faith among psychologists is the reason why the greatest part of their efforts are of no practical value to the world; and the deficiency in Faith among metaphysicians is the reason why all the sick are not healed, why all who have troubles do not secure complete emancipation.

This is one of the greatest truths of all truths, and should not only receive profound attention from every mind, but it is a truth that should be constantly held in every mind. To live, think and act in the spirit of this truth . . the truth that you live and move and have your being in a world of unlimited power and that through Faith all of this power is placed at your command . . to live in this truth, with Faith, is to open the mind more and more to the perpetual influx of this power, until you gain so much of this power that nothing becomes impossible to you henceforth and forever. That there is such a world no one can doubt; that Faith is the hidden path to that world anyone can demonstrate; anyone can also demonstrate that we gain possession of an immense power while we are in that world, and that the power continues to be our own so long as we remain in the full Faith; it is therefore evident that those who will continue permanently in the full Faith will accomplish everything they may undertake to do.

Faith is this practical, literal seeing God (consciousness), Life, Spirit, Substance, right here and now. All must come to this knowledge, from the least to the greatest, in one way or another. If not through conscious aspiration (desire, prayer), then through experience, through "hard lines." "Know the Lord: for all shall know me, from the least to the greatest." According to the degree of your acceptance and use of this Presence, which is active Faith, it is established unto you. If you know God (consciousness) as Life and Harmony, you have Health, you are Health. If you know God (consciousness) as Abundance, you lack no good thing. It depends upon your Faith.

Your Faith Is Your Fortune: Your Unlimited Power

Faith is that something in man that transcends every form of limitation and opens the mind to the limitless powers of the soul. It is Faith that emancipates the person; it is Faith that unfolds the unbounded greatness of the soul; it is Faith that removes the veil of mystery and reveals to man that wonderful world, that limitless world, that divinely beautiful world that is within.

Faith has been the hidden secret of the great souls in every age; Faith has been the secret through which all miracles have been wrought; Faith has been the secret through which the prophet gained his wisdom and his power; Faith has been the secret through which the sons of glory gained their rare and wonderful genius; Faith has been the secret through which everything high, everything worthy and everything beautiful has been given to the world.

It is Faith that the awakened minds have eternally sought to find, though not always knowing that the hidden secret was Faith, and Faith alone; and it is Faith that will change the world, as the world should be changed, when its inner sanctuary has been entered by the mind of man.

Faith is the hidden secret to everything; the key that unlocks every door that may exist in the universe; Faith is the perfect way to that inner world from which all things proceed; Faith is the royal path to unbounded power, immeasurable wisdom and limitless love; Faith is the gates ajar to that kingdom which first must be sought if all other things arc to be added; Faith is the hidden secret to every desire and need of man.

By a right understanding, and by using right thoughts and words, man will regain the kingdom within him and will be reinstated in the Garden of Eden. This process of man's taking up power and dominion again is now being carried out in all those who are seeking the righteousness of the Christ consciousness. In this higher-thought realm, all ideas pertaining to the life of man are in harmonious relation, and when we ask in silent thought for this knowledge, our mind is flooded with its light. We apprehend only according to the receptivity, steadfastness, understanding, and persistent Faith of our mind. But we grow in Faith and understanding, and no matter how slowly we seem to be progressing we should never be discouraged or give up. Everyone is heir to this higher-thought consciousness, and all must eventually attain it. When the beauty of this spiritual realm is spread before us we should express gratitude . . give thanks to the great Soul of the universe. When the astronomer Kepler realized the grandeur of the laws that were revealed to him, he exclaimed: "O God (consciousness), I AM thinking Thy thoughts after Thee."

The life is fullest that is most replete with creative images, that ventures most in Faith into the Unseen but not Unknown. And the dreamer is no longer to be despised. Dream your dreams, see your visions, picture your good, knowing that you draw forth from the inexhaustible resources of heaven just what your Faith demands. Vision and Faith will carry you across every sea of despair, every mountain of difficulty. Ask, with Faith, believing.

Faith is an attitude of mind that turns the superior sense of man towards the inner, the hidden, the unseen, the great beyond, and takes consciousness into those finer realms where everything is perfect, and far more real than that which appears to visible sight. Faith demonstrates that that which seems unreal is absolutely real; that that which seems hidden can be revealed to any mind, and understood by any mind; and that the invisible becomes visible to all those who will open the full vision that exists within them. Faith demonstrates that the inner world is far more substantial than the outer world, and that the farther we proceed into the great within the more substantial, the more real, the more perfect and the more beautiful everything becomes. One of the principal functions of Faith is to enter the boundless and awaken the great within; and since all increase in life, power and ability comes from the awakening of a larger and a larger measure of the within, we understand perfectly why all things are possible to him who has Faith.

All things visible come forth through Faith from the invisible Spirit substance itself. Have Faith in God, (consciousness) actually in him, that is, within him. See your desire in God (consciousness), and know that he manifests as the fulfillment of it. Since God (consciousness) is the omnipresence, he is the source of all things visible and invisible. Being all, God (consciousness) has no consciousness of either lack or possession, only the realization of being all . . all that is. It is his joy, then, to be the fulfillment, or that which fills full, your desire.

Persistency in Faith is like fire under the boiler. Faith generates the Energy necessary to success. There is nothing that cannot be accomplished through Faith. But the trouble with most persons is that they do not hold to their Faith long enough to realize the fulfillment of their desire. They are up today and down tomorrow. Their Faith works by fits and starts. They lack the stick-to-itiveness which brings success. St. James says of such a person: He that wavereth is like a wave of the sea, driven with the wind and tossed. Let not that man think that he shall receive anything of the Lord. The Law says that if we want success we must have Faith and persistency. The promise is that In due season we shall reap if we faint not. The faint heart cripples Faith and limits its capacity for worthwhile achievement. You cannot lose if you hang on.

Faith transforms failure into success. These persons feel that they are in league with the Powers of the universe, and they fear nothing human or diabolic. The forces of environment and heredity, terrible though they be, are broken and driven from the field. Hope takes the place of despair, and the energies of a new life reach out in every direction.

All things that are seen have been made of the substance of Faith. "Faith is the substance of things hoped for, the evidence of things not seen." The very worlds were brought forth through Faith by the word of God (consciousness) so that "Things which are seen were not made of things which do appear." All things are made of the invisible substance of God (consciousness), "framed by the word" through the power of Faith. When you frame a picture, you outline it, or enclose it in its frame. Even so do you frame, or outline, your desire by the word you speak. What Faith pictures have you been outlining, or framing, by the power of your word? Have these pictures been of Faith or of fear? There is a law of fear as well as a law of Faith. Job found that what he feared came upon him. He had framed in mind a fearful picture, and it became manifest. The Master said, "Fear not, only believe" for it was his desire that man should know he could frame ideal conditions through the power of the word and so experience freedom instead of bondage.

Fear is the shadow side of Faith. It works against you rather than for you. Therefore, fear not, believe only. Let all your force be used in believing. Waste none of it in fear. Have Faith only . . no fear at all. Fear is born of untruth, believing in the power and presence of evil. The truth is, God (consciousness) is all and he is good. He is the only power, substance and intelligence. Have Faith in God (consciousness), the good. Fear is negative and creates every negative condition. It brings undesirable things only. Faith is positive and creates positive conditions. It brings all that is good and desirable. "Faith is the substance of things hoped for," or desired. Desire that which is good, then have Faith. It is to be formed of the very substance of your own Faith, for Faith is substance . . mind substance.

This is one of the greatest truths of all truths, and should not only receive profound attention from every mind, but it is a truth that should be constantly held in every mind. To live, think and act in the spirit of this truth . . the truth that you live and move and have your being in a world of unlimited power and that through Faith all of this power is placed at your command . . to live in this truth, with Faith, is to open the mind more and more to the perpetual influx of this power, until you gain so much of this power that nothing becomes impossible to you henceforth and forever. That there is such a world no one can doubt; that Faith is the hidden path to that world anyone can demonstrate; anyone can also demonstrate that we gain possession of an immense power while we are in that world, and that the power continues to be our own so long as we remain in the full Faith; it is therefore evident that those who will continue permanently in the full Faith will accomplish everything they may undertake to do.

God (consciousness) himself has given you the power of Faith. It is a law. It is a law which he has given to make you free. Until you use the law of Faith you are in bondage to every earthly condition; but once you become conscious of the "Faith that worketh by love," you are forever free. Knowledge of freedom through the law of Faith is one of the great gifts given to the world by the Master. How he plead with man to use it!

Lack of health is not prevalent in God's (consciousness's) universe. If such lack appears anywhere it is the work of man. It is our duty to do away with it. There is something wrong in a world where suffering and sorrow prevail. We would not create such a world. We all want to see these things blotted out in this world. This is the index pointing the way to the possibility of doing so. Just accept the promises of Scripture. Proceed to carry them out in Faith. Act as if they were true. Trust God (consciousness) in all things. Whatever we see as wrong is for us to right. The new Christianity elevates man to a realm in which seeming miracles of healing become possible to those who train their mind to think spiritually.

Faith is not something which lies outside the self, but a consciousness within the self. Everyone has Faith, but few recognize it, and only the very few know how to use it, and what it can accomplish. The Master made no limit to the power of Faith. "If ye have Faith as a grain of mustard seed . . . nothing shall be impossible unto you/' That Faith lies within the individual, he clearly indicates in the following: "Thy Faith hath made thee whole." "According to your Faith be it unto you." Again, he asked, "Where is your Faith?" At another time he questioned them in wonderment, "How is it that ye have no Faith?" Thus we see the first evidences of Faith are to be found within the individual. It is there in some form, and it is always exercised though often unconsciously. Now that we are learning the wonders that may be produced through Faith, it is time to awaken to its presence within us and to exercise this power until it accomplishes for us the works we wish it to do.

WHAT ARE THE SIX STEPS IN DEMONSTRATION?

The first step is to formulate our desire . . to see it clearly in Mind. The second step is to impress it with deep feeling upon the Subconscious Mind, to see ourselves accomplishing that thing. The third step is to exercise our Faith by accepting the desire as fulfilled. The fourth step is to keep our feeling and thinking moving with our desire. The fifth step is to order our conversation aright . . to speak always in terms of expectancy and fulfillment. The sixth step is to carry our desire into action . . to act as if it were already fulfilled.

Rise in consciousness to the level of your desire and make yourself one with it by claiming it to be so now. Have Faith in this unseen claim until the conviction is born within you that it is so. Your confidence in this claim will pay great rewards. Just a little while and he, the thing desired, will come. But without Faith, it is impossible to realize anything. Through Faith, the worlds were framed, because "Faith is the substance of the thing hoped for – the evidence of the thing not yet seen"

As the unmanifest and uncreate Being, which fills the universe, is all life, all law, substance and power, all Mind, Principle or Spirit, it is axiomatic that, if we speak the truth which frees, we are to speak the word of the all; therefore, as all Being is uncreate, all life, law, substance and power are unmanifest, silent and invisible, until through thought they are spoken and made manifest. To base our Faith aright is to base it in the unseen and Unmanifest Spirit; and as it is the only Being, we cannot be Faithful but by speaking its word; and, as there is but one Cause or Creator, to speak the word of the one is to speak the word of all, and that word is truth to each one at all times, and in every place. To base our Faith in material things, things that are seen, is to base it in effect or shadow, which is neither life, law, substance nor power. As temporal things pass away, the foundation upon which we have builded is as sand; disappointment, sorrow and pain follow such building, as the wheels of the carriage follow him who draws the carriage. We are to realize that the unseen, uncreate Spirit of Goodness, is that which creates and manifests all; so, if our Faith be based aright, we shall place ourselves in thought at one with Spirit, and work to manifest the Faith of Spirit.

Since Faith is the hidden secret of all life, and is absolutely indispensable to existence, we all have Faith just as we all have life; to find Faith, we are therefore not required to search for something we never knew; we are simply required to have more Faith in the Faith we already possess; the greater things will invariably follow.

Fear, humility, love, trust, remorse, the joy of reconciliation, the pain of estrangement, are all emotional states. Moreover, there is a vast and half-explored background of vague feeling which fades away into the subconscious, a reservoir of life behind consciousness, which seems as if it might be the very soil out of which Faith springs and grows. If we could tap this subliminal self, and force it to give up its secrets, should we not find our Faith definite, explicit, and self-sufficing?

Through the growth of Faith . . the real Faith, the mind becomes more and more aware of this inner world, and consciousness opens more and more to receive its limitless power; the entire personality becomes filled with the power, and before long you feel that an immense power is with you every moment of existence. This brings the realization that nothing is impossible; you never hesitate to undertake anything that is worthy, no matter how great and extensive the undertaking may be, because you know there is a power with you that can do all things. You feel that this power is working through you; you feel that it is your power; therefore, anything worthy that you may undertake, the same shall be done. To enter this realization is to gain more power from the very beginning; therefore, he who enters Faith will begin at once to accomplish greater things and better things, whatever his work may be; and as for his future, it is as great, as wonderful and as beautiful as he may desire to make it.

The blessing of health comes through the exercise of Faith on the part of the man who seeks it. Faith opens the mind to the influx of power from on high. The power of the Highest heals all diseases both of soul and of body. When Faith is sufficiently strong to dissolve all adverse conditions and to open the mind fully to the power of God (consciousness), healing is instantaneous. Through Faith in the reality of things spiritual we begin soul evolution. We must have Faith in Spirit and through our thinking build it into our consciousness. Then our body will be restored to harmony and health. In order to create as God (consciousness) creates, man must have undoubting Faith in God-Mind (his own consciousness) and the obedience of the creative electrons hidden in the atoms of all substance. Although we all get definite results in body and affairs from the words we utter, those results would be infinitely greater if we understood the power of words and had undoubting Faith in their creative power.

Experience has convinced me that an assumption, though false, if persisted in, will harden into fact, that continuous imagination is sufficient for all things, and all my reasonable plans and actions will never make up for my lack of continuous imagination. Is it not true that the teachings of the Gospels can only be received in terms of Faith and that the Son of God (consciousness) is constantly looking for signs of Faith in people . . that is, Faith in their own imagination?

Give Faith to everything, have Faith in everything, unite Faith with everything, and everything shall be filled with that power that makes all things possible. If you wish to reach the highest places that life has in store for man have Faith, and your wish shall positively come true. It is Faith that awakens the higher and greater within you, thereby elevating all your faculties to the highest state of efficiency; it is Faith that opens the mind to that superior power that alone can create the prodigy and the genius; it is Faith that gives such a rare quality to everything you do that both you and your work are stamped universally with the mark of high worth.

Faith is not belief. Belief may change. Faith does not change for it knows that which is so. Faith does not argue, or question, or waver, or hesitate. Faith knows. Today you may have a certain belief. Tomorrow your belief may be strengthened into a hope that it may be as you believe, but when you demonstrate the belief that your hope may be true, you will have the Faith that knows it is true, and because it is so, it will so manifest. This is the Faith that heals the sick, raises the dead, rebukes the devil, removes the mountains, and sets you free. The Faith that does this work comes only from understanding your right to exercise it.

It doesn't matter how small your Faith is, if you believe in it, if you have Faith in it, if you keep it alive, if you keep it in motion, it has to grow. Never allow yourself to minimize your "mustard seed" of Faith. Never allow yourself to think of your Faith as inadequate. Know that you have it and that you couldn't lose it if you wanted to. Praise it. Let it grow. It will do wonders for you; nothing shall be impossible to you.

There is a world of limitless power; that world is within us and all about us, but in ordinary consciousness we are not aware of its existence; at those times, however, when we transcend ordinary consciousness we gain glimpses of this marvelous world. It is during such moments that we feel strong enough to move mountains; it is then that we receive our inspirations, when new truths are revealed, when new discoveries are made, and when immortal deeds are done. This world of limitless power is an inner world permeating the outer world, and is revealed through Faith; it is through Faith that we enter into this world, and it is through the growth of Faith that we realize its limitless power, thereby gaining possession of a greater measure of this power.

The mustard seed Faith is not a small Faith, as many have supposed. The Master in speaking of it referred to its quality rather than its quantity. The Faith of the mustard seed is, that being a mustard seed, it has the right to give expression to the mustard plant. It is this kind of a Faith, this same quality, that man is expected to use. He is to know that being a Son of God (consciousness) he has the right to express all that the Son of God (consciousness) is, the fullness, the freedom, the power and perfection of his being. Man, the offspring of God (consciousness), who is indeed the very image and likeness of God (consciousness), has been given dominion in earth. He does not exercise it consciously, and so fails to produce for himself the harmonious environment he should enjoy. Instead, not knowing his right to exercise this power, he unconsciously subjects himself to every form of inharmony and imperfection because through doubt and fear he brings their reaction upon him. Man has dominion in earth. Earth responds to his exercise of that dominion. Fearful things shape themselves as the result of fear. Faithfully the perfect takes form at the exercise of Faith. The substance of earth as readily responds to man's call for the full and complete expression of his idea, as it does to the call of the mustard seed when it determines to express itself. "It is indeed the least of all seeds; but when it is grown, it is the greatest among herbs, and becometh a tree, so that the birds of the air come and lodge in the branches thereof." When man understands the possibility that lies in his right of dominion, he will do the mighty work that it is his privilege to do.

The best way to prove that all wisdom and all understanding are in man is just to believe it to be true. Coming into the Christ consciousness is, in its first steps, all a matter of Faith. The intellect, sense mind, thinks that it could understand if only somebody would explain Truth to it; but it never seems to understand. The best way to prove this is to take some statement of Truth that is not clear. Hold it in mind. The power of the word will quicken the understanding, and light will flash from within. This is spiritual knowing. Believe in the quickening power of the word. Hold the word in mind. It will reveal itself, for wrapped in the word is its meaning, and you, being the image and likeness of God (consciosuness), can understand it if you make connection with it in your inner consciousness. By planting it in consciousness and waiting for its fruit, anyone can prove that the word is seed.

When we have Faith in all people we attract better people, and will have the privilege to live with those who are as we wish them to be. What we constantly hold in mind that we invariably attract to ourselves; and receives our undivided attention. We shall consequently have the privilege to associate with those who express the real and the true in the highest and most perfect measure. He who has the most Faith in mankind has the most friends and the best friends; he receives the truest love from the largest number, and the best that the world can give will constantly flow into his life.

Knowing your desire exists in your imagination, simply expect its fulfillment in your outer world. Try it. I have lived by this law all of my life and know, that by applying this principle, all of your desires will be fulfilled. The law operates by Faith. If you believe, no effort is necessary to see the fulfillment of your every desire.

Have Faith to know God (consciousness) is, Faith to ask because God (consciousness) is, Faith to receive because God (consciousness) is, and Faith to act believing that you have already received, . . this is a full Faith. The Father indeed knoweth that you have need of all these things, but the Father desires your recognition of him. He desires that you shall look to him, see him as the beginning, and as the fulfillment of your desire. Therefore, he bids you "Ask." He tells you plainly in the words of the Master that it will be unto thee "as thou wilt." He would have you know that he will satisfy the hunger of your heart, but also he would have you understand that "He that cometh to him must believe that he is and that he is a rewarder of them that diligently seek him."

Faith opens all the doors to everything that mind may desire to secure; Faith opens the mind to that immense inner world from which everything may be received. It is being demonstrated more fully every day that all things pertaining to the life of man come from the within; not only great things, but all things. From the within comes all wisdom, and the mind that has awakened the largest measure of their within has the greatest wisdom.

God (consciousness) (your awareness) is not mocked. You are ever receiving that which you are aware of being and no man gives thanks for something which he has not received. "Thank You, Father" is not, as it is used by many today, a sort of magical formula. You need never utter aloud the words, "Thank You, Father". In applying this principle, as you rise in consciousness to the point where you are really grateful and happy for having received the thing desired, you automatically rejoice and give thanks inwardly. You have already accepted the gift which was but a desire before you rose in consciousness, and your Faith is now the substance that shall clothe your desire.

Through Faith every desire can be realized, and every object in view can be accomplished, because Faith places mind in touch with the power that can do all things. Faith opens the mind to the unbounded power from within and creates in mind the conscious realization of that power. When you are in Faith the power that you feel is so great that nothing seems impossible; you feel strong enough to do almost anything, and what you feel is the truth. You can do anything while you are absolutely in Faith, because while you are in Faith you are in a world where unlimited power is at your command.

When you have obligations to meet, bills to pay, and have not the essentials required, have Faith; never worry nor feel anxious for a moment; know that Faith can open to you the realms of limitless supply, and know that Faith will do this if you have Faith in Faith. Whatever you need place the matter in the hands of Faith; Faith will find a way; Faith will reveal to you the necessary opportunities through which you may accomplish what you desire and meet your obligations. Do not ask how, simply depend upon Faith; you will soon know how; have Faith in Faith and the hidden secrets of Faith will be fully revealed to you. Never be disturbed if results should fail to appear at once; know that Faith will open the way before it is too late; and the same shall positively be done. Again, we must remember not to depend simply upon a mere belief in Faith, but to mentally dwell in the very soul of Faith.

It has been sufficiently shown that, in spite of theological claims to the contrary, Faith is not a faculty by itself, acting apart from the understanding. It is merely a function or mode of operation of the governing faculty of reason, though in its results less certain than the process of inference, because dealing with objects the existence of which cannot be verified. It is precisely because knowledge of the unknown is not available that Faith has appropriated it as its own peculiar province.

When we enter the inner spirit of Faith we discover that there is a higher power in man, and all about the being of man; in brief, we live and move in an infinite sea of higher power. No matter how far we may go in the ascending scale of life, there is always a higher power that we may realize and appropriate for personal, tangible use. To gain possession of this higher power, Faith is the secret; because Faith transcends all limitations; Faith perpetually transcends; therefore, to live in Faith is to pass eternally from the superior to that which is greater than the superior; from that which seems limitless to that which is infinitely larger and more sublime. In the mind of the average person there is a belief that he is a limited personality, endowed with a certain amount of physical and menial energy; he believes that there is no way to increase that amount, therefore, stamps upon the subconscious the idea of the limitation he has fixed for himself. The result is that he receives from the limitless source only as much power as his limited, circumscribed mentality can receive and appropriate; he is not aware of the fact that what he does receive comes from the limitless source; nor does he know that the supply received is limited simply because he thinks that his power is limited. The law is that we receive from the source of limitless power only as much power as we think we possess; therefore, by expanding consciousness so as to realize a larger measure of power we begin to receive this larger measure.

Faith, absolute dogmatic Faith, is the only law of true success. When we recognize the fact that a man carries his success or his failure with him, and that it does not depend upon outside conditions, we will come into the possession of powers that will quickly change outside conditions into agencies that make for success. When we come into this higher realization and bring our lives into complete harmony with the higher laws, we will then be able so to focus and direct the awakened interior forces, that they will go out and return laden with that for which they are sent. We will then be great enough to attract success, and it will not always be apparently just a little ways ahead. We can then establish in ourselves a center so strong that instead of running hither and thither for this or that, we can stay at home and draw to us the conditions we desire. If we firmly establish and hold to this centre, things will seem continually to come our way.

Faith awakens the new life, the healing life, the emancipating life, the purifying life, the regenerating life, the life that is power, health, wholeness and freedom; therefore, through Faith anyone may attain complete emancipation from all the ills of human existence.

Faith is the perceiving power of the mind linked with the power to shape substance. It is spiritual assurance. It is the power to do the seemingly impossible. It is a magnetic power that draws unto us our heart's desire from the invisible spiritual substance. Faith is a deep inner knowing that that which is sought is already ours for the taking.

As Being, (the Christ) divine man knows he contacts, and is within himself one with the power, substance and intelligence of which and through which things are given form. Through the prophetic power of Being, (Elias) man prophesies, foretells, or conceives the form which his power, substance and intelligence shall express. Through the law of mind, (Moses) which the divine intelligence of Being exercises, man brings forth through Faith that which he has conceived, and "according to his Faith," or in the exact pattern of his belief, he then has in tangible form, that which before he had only in an unmanifest state. Fulfilling the law of mind, brings the unmanifest into manifestation, or causes it to materialize.

Assume now that you have all the Faith in God (consciousness) that you need. Then act in accordance with this assumption. Every affirmation, thought, feeling, word and action that expresses Faith impresses Faith upon the inner mind. As the subconscious accepts the impression, it will set in motion forces that are Faith-producing. When we fill the Subconscious Mind with Faith . . thoughts of Faith, feelings of Faith, memories of acts of Faith . . by some mechanism of creation, we have Faith. The Law of Action and Reaction is at work. The impression is an act of Faith; the reaction expresses the power of Faith. The Subconscious Mind is the creative phase of Mind. The Subconscious Mind acts on what is given to it but does not originate anything. But not every thought and feeling penetrates to the Subconscious fortunately. We cannot always determine which of the many impressions we receive in the course of the day will go beyond the conscious Mind . . the Mind of the senses . . the top of the Mind. Whatever passes through this Mind and finds lodging in the subjective Mind is quite likely to be pregnant with feeling of some kind.

Our first step in demonstration is to contact God (consciousness). We then have the fullness of God's (consciousness's) wisdom, love and truth (or power, substance and intelligence) with us in bringing it forth. Our work is to begin from the I AM in us which is one with the I AM that is in all, and all in all. A leaf on a vine begins its expression at that point within itself wherein it is joined to the whole vine . . its stem. This is the door through which the expression of the vine comes forth into the leaf. Even so within us is the "door," the Christ within, the I AM in our consciousness which contacts the great I AM that is the life and light of all.

Your expression is to be given forth from within you, even as the leaf unfolds from within itself. Your affairs are to be operated from within you. "But thou, when thou prayest, enter into thy closet (the inner sanctuary of the soul) and when thou hast shut thy door, pray to thy Father which is in secret; and thy Father which seeth in secret shall reward thee openly." The first and greatest commandment, the Master said, is this important thing of making complete at-one-ment with the Father within. He gave it in the following words:

"Thou shalt love the Lord thy God (law of consciousness) with all thy heart, with all thy soul, with all thy strength and with all thy mind."

Do you not see how you must be centered in the Father (consciousness) within you, drawing the whole of your good from him, and that every force of your nature is to operate from the divine self? "In the beginning" of all expression is God (consciousness), the God (consciousness) within, else God (consciousness)could not be expressed, or brought forth.

Truly, "the things that are seen are not made of that which doth appear!" "Faith is the substance of things hoped for, the evidence of things not seen." "Whatsoever things ye desire when ye pray, believe that ye have received them and ye ' shall receive them." Out of the invisible realms of spirit, out of that which from the physical side is "nothing" but which from the spiritual side is "everything," out of that nothing into which science can entirely dissolve matter, and yet from which all matter proceeds, man may draw his good by simply repeating the creative process; and this is the work of vision. You need have no fear for the issue, if you will but have Faith in the power of visualization. Let your soul articulate in form. Perceive your good inwardly and claim it. If it is money you need, see yourself in possession of it. If it is a journey you wish to take, then venture out in vision. Visualize the trip; go to Paris while still in London; visit Rome while still in Paris. But do not rest there. State firmly and with conviction, " This is the picture of what is mine. Let it be brought forth in a completeness which is above my present scope of vision." Then it "shall be done unto you above all you ask or think."

When we direct the mental powers upon a definite idea, Faith plays its part. It is involved in concentration. As we give attention to the idea through one-pointed mind concentration, we break into a realm of finer mind activity.

The Son in man embodies all the creative possibility of the Father. "As the Father hath life in himself, so hath he given unto the Son to have life in himself," said Jesus. This understanding gives man immovable Faith, enables him to know that he has all power within, and thus gives him the courage to make use of it. He finds that within his own being he is the very power, substance and intelligence out of which, and because of which, all things are given form, and that "All things, whatsoever," can be made to take form, and do take form, in the exact pattern of the form he holds in mind, or visions. There is but one limit to man's power and that is the limit in his own consciousness of power, which prevents him from thinking into manifestation the farm he desires. Power and substance in mind as definitely bring forth man's conception as do sun and earth bring forth the flower hidden within the seed when it is cast into the ground. Man is safe with this consciousness for it cannot be fully unfolded to him until he has entered into love. He may express the high psychic, or prophetic power, but unless that power is used in love, it "bites back," as does the serpent, and he must cry out for deliverance. Love is the great deliverer. Christ is supreme power, and Christ in man has all power, because he understands that all power is God (consciousness), and that he is one with God (consciousness), sent of God (consciousness) to be "about his Father's business" of freeing all mankind from bondage. He fears no lack. He knows no limitation. Any mountain of obstruction in the way must dissolve before that mustard seed quality of consciousness which knows its right to express itself . . the living Christ within.

Faith is scientific. It cannot fail to demonstrate. It is definite principle, impersonal in its nature. Neither worthiness nor unworthiness on the part of the one using it enters into the consideration of what Faith will do. The law of Faith is as definite a principle as that of mathematics. A thief may add and subtract, multiply and divide. A philanthropist may do the same. Even so, the law of Faith is open for the use of all. Universal principle is for universal use. "He maketh his sun to rise on the evil and the good, and sendeth his rain on the just and the unjust." Misuse of any law brings upon the one so using it the reaction of the law. The law itself causes neither happiness nor unhappiness. It is the use of the law which produces effects. Untrue motives bring unhappy experiences. True motives bring forth that which is good and true. The actor is always responsible for the act. "A good tree bringeth forth good fruit, but a corrupt tree bringeth forth evil fruit." Both, however, produce by the same law. The law of Faith will bring forth for those who use it. Without fail, it will give to the one applying it that for which he asks, and exactly that for which he asks.

When Faith seems to fail, have more Faith; and have more Faith in Faith; you will thereby produce a turn in the lane, because Faith can produce anything; Faith opens the mind to limitless power, therefore, we can never doubt the power of Faith.

In the same way the Master met the devil, or false belief, of taxation when it was presented. He did not allow himself, or his disciples, to be limited by taxes, but called upon the larger consciousness of freedom, and taught them how to prove themselves greater than taxes. Reminding Peter of the truth of freedom, the Master lifted his consciousness above limitation, and sent him to the sea (representing the universal source in which all things have their beginning) to obtain the tribute money from the mouth of the fish that should first come to him. "The Sons of God (consciousness) are free." They are greater than any limitation which the unenlightened may endeavor to press upon them. Those in Christ consciousness whimper no more. They can give two fold for all that is required of them. In universal consciousness, they are free, can meet any obligation, "lest they offend" those who do not as yet understand. Every mountain in your objective thought which seems to deny freedom to the Christ within is to be cast into the great universal God (consciousness) mind, and there it will be dissolved, or removed from your pathway without harm to any and without resistance on your part. You, however, must know your power to cast it there, and speak your word of authority . . "Remove hence to yonder place." Then will it remove. Such is the law.

The law of Faith is a creative law. It brings forth. It must then begin its operation in the creative center . . God (consciousness). As a creative law, it must be considered in such light. As a universal law it has universal application on whatever plane of consciousness it is operating. Sun and earth bring forth a flower when the seed is planted in earth. Father and mother bring forth a child when the conception' takes place within the mother. Spirit and soul bring forth expression in body and affairs when the seed-idea underlying that expression is planted, or conceived within the soil of the soul. This, briefly stated, is the law. Sun and earth are impersonal in their productive capacities, bringing forth Whatever seed is planted, the choice of the seed lying with the individual who desires the plant. We shall someday understand that rare children are born of parents of rare and idealistic consciousness, and that souls born upon the earth seek their own level of mind unfoldment. Unconsciously parents choose their offspring by the quality of their own thought. Spirit and soul are equally impersonal in their creative possibilities. "The desire of thine heart" is brought forth. Things are shaped in your experience "according to your Faith." God (consciousness) is no respecter of persons. The law is the law. "God (consciousness) hath committed all judgment unto the Son". That is, God (consciousness) allows man to judge for himself as to what shall take place in his life, . . the perfection God (consciousness) has conceived for him, or the bitter experiences which shall cause him finally to cry out for the perfection. Every seed idea placed in the soul becomes a conception, is given thought-form in mind, later to be experienced in physical form. Ideas of perfection produce perfection. The reverse is equally true. Just as sun and earth produce with equal willingness the mighty oak and the frailest poppy when their respective seeds are planted, so spirit and soul respond to the call of man, and that which he desires, or for which he has asked, believing, he receives.

The greater the Faith the larger the view and the better the view, whatever the subject of thought may be; and the more thorough the understanding. Faith is therefore a priceless gift to every mind in existence; for there is no place in life where Faith will not be a great and wonderful power for good. Through Faith the mind ascends into that state of being where the life more abundant . . the spiritual life, the eternal life . . is realized and received; and among all the powers of Faith, this is the greatest. The unfoldment of the inner life prepares the way for the unfoldment of the soul, and places every high spiritual attainment within reach of the growing mind.

The law represents the first plane of conscious power man attains. It is this that leads him out of sense darkness into a higher state of mind, that which reveals psychic, or prophetic power. This is a wilderness state of consciousness, for terrible reactions result from a misuse of this power through lack of knowledge as to its highest purpose. Here man is "bit by the serpent," psychic reaction, until he learns to "lift it up," then he is led out of it into the "promised land," the full Christ consciousness wherein man is given dominion over every condition and stands supreme. Christ is greater than the law and the prophets, and every man is to unfold through these planes until he reaches Christ consciousness and uses both law and prophecy to bring forth his divine ideas into expression.

If you can fill your Mind with the precious qualities of courage, confidence, and Faith, nothing can defeat you. When the Subconscious Mind gets a new idea (when the idea takes possession of the conscious Mind), it gets you. When you empty the Subconscious of all adverse, tense, troublesome, and distorted thoughts and fill it with thoughts of life, power, victory, and optimism, the whole tenor of your life will change. "But this is such tedious work," you say. That is right, but so is anything that is worthwhile and lasting. Don't be misled by the printed or spoken word. Many people say to me after listening to a lecture, "It sounds so easy when you tell us about it," and I know that is true. Faith is easy to understand but hard to apply.

When we have achieved spiritual realization of our prayer and our innermost soul is satisfied, we have the assurance that the thing is accomplished in Spirit and must become manifest. We may continue in our realization of Faith until the whole consciousness responds and the instantaneous demonstration takes place. Prayer is impotent and unfruitful when the one who prays is without the firm belief that his prayers are answered. When man turns wholeheartedly to God (consciousness), the prayer of Faith brings forth abundantly. Since the prayer of Faith is the activity of divine love, let us pray without ceasing, knowing that God (consciousness) hears and grants our petitions.

Through the outworking of the law of Faith we grow like that which we gaze upon, or hold in mind for ourselves. This law of Faith, or suggestion, is very potent, but it becomes doubly so when that which is suggested to us is something we love, or idealize. Grecian mothers were very careful to surround themselves with every ideal influence during the months prior to the birth of their children, and Paul who understood this law emphasized it in speaking of the Christ ideal, . . "We all with open face beholding as in a glass the glory of the Lord, are changed into the same image from glory to glory." The Old Testament story of Jacob, who placed the spotted sticks in the drinking water of his cows, is but another illustration of the subtle power of this law. The cows brought forth that which they gazed upon, . . potted offsprings after the pattern of the spotted sticks they saw in the water day by day.

The drinking water but typifies the water of the soul which God (consciousness) always "moves upon" in order to bring forth. Here is reflected and conceived the divine idea which is to be held in mind, and brought to birth in outer form. When the water of the soul is kept as still as that of a placid lake the reflection is perfect, and the divine idea becomes clear and well defined in mind. As we gaze upon it, love it, hold it as our ideal, and desire to bring it forth, in fullness of time it is given birth and that which we cherished in mind takes actual form.

Therefore be firm, in speaking the word of truth for healing. Affirm that which is true in Being by speaking the true word which will unlock the inner kingdom of reality and establish its ideas in experience. When the word for the true condition has been spoken, claim the effect of that word, and be unmoved by any appearance to the contrary. From the moment the word of Truth is spoken, claim its full fruition, believing that you have received, and act in perfect accord with that belief. Action must carry out the spirit of the mind, . . not contradict it. It is this that builds the house, or establishes the body, so that nothing from without can affect it. From the moment you speak the word "health," hold it in mind, and act as though health is already received for in this way is the law of Faith fulfilled. Regardless of every appearance, claim that health is yours from the moment you ask the Father within to manifest as health, for the Father within, or this Infinite Power in the Heaven within, can no more avoid responding than the sound within the piano can help coming forth when the key is struck. For this reason it is written, "If you ask for bread, will he give you a stone?" He cannot give you a stone, for it is the nature of the Father to give you that for which you ask. "Ask and you shall receive, for everyone that asketh, receiveth."

Thoughts of themselves become things, and every mental attitude produces an effect of some kind. We are therefore constantly demonstrating the thing we do not want by thinking how much we do not want it. The bad that comes to us is simply the expression of wrong thinking. Malignant diseases are as much a matter of demonstration as their cure. A "cure" does not deal with the disease. It has nothing to do with the disease. The true healer never thinks," I am healing disease." He says, "I AM knowing the truth." The disease, which is the expression of your Faith in disease, vanishes before your Faith in health.

To secure the largest and best possible results from the practical application of Faith, it is necessary to have a perfect Faith in everything with which we may come in contact, both on the visible and invisible sides of life. Have Faith in yourself, have Faith in man, have Faith in the universe, have Faith in God (consciousness), and have Faith in Faith. To have Faith in everything is to develop the power of Faith in every direction, and it is the full Faith that opens the mind to the power that can do all things. The principal reason why Faith sometimes fails is because we exercise Faith in some things while we have doubts about others. It is the Faith that has Faith in all things and at all times that is real Faith; and it is the Faith that has Faith in the full Faith that makes all things possible. When we have Faith in all things we enter into absolute oneness with the real life of all things; we place ourselves in touch with the universal, and may consequently draw upon the limitless for anything the heart may desire.

In the Heart of man's being, where he is one with the Father, the Father says, "I AM that power, substance and intelligence which is the fulfillment of your every desire."

In Soul, the question is asked, "What do you desire?" In Mind, it is required, "Believe ye have that which ye desire." In Expression, it is promised, "And ye shall have the fulfillment of your desire."

As has been before stated, this is a creative law, the law of bringing forth, and in operation is exactly the same as that used upon the physical plane when father and mother conceive a child, the body of which is given form within the matrix of the mother, and in fullness of time is brought to birth. Even so the Spirit (father) and Soul (mother) conceive what is to be brought forth, and this seed-idea is held within the matrix of the soul, the mind, until in fullness of time it is produced in form, or delivered upon the physical plane.

It is now easy to see that your desire in the without must through "the silence," or in prayer be carried to the inner sanctuary of the soul ("thy closet") and there placed as a definite request before the Father . . the I AM. This is "asking." The Spirit asks, "What shall I do for thee?" You answer by naming your desire, . . by asking.

Lifted to the spiritual plane, your request is there quickened by the Spirit and becomes a conception in your soul. Now it is a conceived idea, . . a seed planted in the soil of your soul. As any other seed, it will germinate, develop first in the invisible, and in "fullness of time" come forth.

The mind, conscious of this, expects the fulfillment, as does a mother her child, or a farmer his harvest. This is "believing." It is "holding in mind" the form of the perfected expression. The mother believes she has her child, even when it is being formed in the invisible. The farmer believes he has his harvest, even while it is growing beneath the soil. We must "believe we have" our demonstration while it is being formed for us in the inner realms of consciousness, for it is "believing we have" that holds definitely in mind the form of our desire, and gives it the desired form. When we believe we have, seeing in Faith, "the invisible," we have.

In fullness of time, this thought form is delivered upon the physical plane. As a mother's birth effort delivers her child, so you through physical effort perfect your demonstration. It requires strength to speak and act in a way that is true to the conception, and to carry out the idea held in mind. The idea of health and the thought form of health must not be denied by the action of sickness or by resorting to external means to try to get well. The thought form is perfect health now.

If the soul conception is abundance, the action must carry out that idea. The spirit of the action must conform to the image. Until abundance manifests the amount of expenditure need not be increased, but the spirit of the mind must be one of richness, and what is spent must be allowed to leave the hands cheerfully and willingly in no consciousness of loss or of self-denial, but rather in the attitude of trust and thanksgiving because of the ever present supply now being made manifest. Be true. Spirit, soul, mind and body must agree to bring forth even as you have conceived, exactly "according to your Faith." "Ye shall reap in due time (the time of fulfillment) if ye faint not. "Be not Faithless, but believing.

It is the man or the woman who lacks Faith and who as a consequence is weakened and crippled by fears and forebodings, who is the creature of all passing occurrences. What one lives in his invisible, thought world, he is continually actualizing in his visible, material world. If he would have any conditions different in the latter he must make the necessary change in the former. A clear realization of this great fact would bring success to thousands of men and women who all about us are now in the depths of despair. It would bring health, abounding health and strength to thousands now diseased and suffering. It would bring peace and joy to thousands now unhappy and ill at ease.

Faith is the hidden secret to the power that can do all things; therefore, to have Faith in Faith is to enter the hidden life of that power; to feel the very spirit of that life, and to permeate that spirit with every conscious action of mind. When we realize that Faith is the hidden secret, and enter into the innermost life of that secret with every thought we think, the invincible powers within will awaken at once; and whatever we desire to do, the same will be done.

Mankind feels his inherent right to freedom and rebels against limitation, but unconscious of the law that will produce it for him, he struggles in the outer world, seeking to get from without, that which can be brought forth only from within. Desires may be fulfilled, and the desire itself is the first step toward the fulfillment. "Woe unto you who are satisfied," cried the Master, who sorrowed because of the woeful ignorance of man and his unwillingness to be delivered from it. "Delight thyself also in the Lord; and he shall give thee the desires of thine heart." "All things, whatsoever, ye desire, when ye pray, believe ye receive them and ye shall have them." "Seek and ye shall find; knock and it shall be opened unto you." These are true promises, and are given to bring happiness and completeness into the lives of men. "Hitherto, ye have asked nothing in my name (in the consciousness of the Son). Ask, and ye shall receive that your joy may be full." You may have what you want, but you must learn that what you want has its beginning in God (consciousness), and you must definitely form your desire in your own consciousness, place it before your Father in the secret place of the Most High (the creative God-center (consciousness) within yourself) and await the action of this Creator in bringing it forth. Ask the Father for what you want. That which begins in God (consciousness) is always good. If you can lay your request before this Perfect One, you need have no fear of its being a good desire, nor of its perfect forthcoming. "He that cometh to God (consciousness) must believe that he is, and that he is a rewarder of them that diligently seek him."

We must think life, talk life, and see ourself filled with the fullness of life. When we are not manifesting life as we desire, it is because our thoughts and our conversation are not in accord with the life idea. Every time we think life, speak life, rejoice in life, we are setting free, and bringing into expression in ourself, more and more of the life idea. Here is the place of abundant life, and we can fill both mind and body, both our surroundings and our affairs, with glad, free, buoyant life by exercising Faith in it.

In every vocation, in every study and in every field of thought, there are new worlds of unbounded possibilities, which when discovered and developed will add immeasurably to the real worth of life. Never yearn for new worlds to conquer, nor complain because there are no opportunities at hand for you; there are a million worlds . . rich, marvelous worlds at your very door; turn your attention to these and you shall have opportunities without number, not simply for the present, but for ages yet to be. The hidden secret to these new worlds is Faith; enter Faith and a new universe shall be given to you; a universe that is more real and substantial than anything you have known before; a universe that is marvelous in beauty, and filled with possibilities more numerous than the sands of the shore.

To hold in mind the ideal is to form the ideal through the operation of the law of Faith; and to free yourself from conditions that are less than ideal, you must cease to hold them in mind, for so long as they are held in mind they are held in experience. For this reason, you can dismember, or bring to nothingness every false condition in experience through remembering it no more, and in its stead form in mind, or establish in consciousness, the perfect condition to be brought forth. When you understand this as a law through which all form becomes manifest, then you will realize how important it is to have Faith in the good. It is for this reason that we ask the Father within for what we want, and by believing that we have received, we have, for it takes form in our experience when we call it forth through asking and believing.

With every demonstration you make, your Faith will be nourished, vitalized, and strengthened. You will come eventually to the place at which you will make your demonstrations easily and naturally. You will build up within your Consciousness a magnetic field which will attract all the elements and factors needed for your success.

The little crocus which so fearlessly braves the cold and frost of early springtime, and through its sweet presence, announces "The winter is over and gone," is one of nature's most precious messengers of the law of Faith and of the possibilities which lie open to man when he will realize and use that law.

The cold and frost of winter become so unbearable to the crocus that it is forced to turn from earth and look longingly upward, believing that somewhere there must be the warmth and cheer which its heart so craves. This call for warmth comes from within itself. It feels the inner urge. It desires good cheer. Every evidence of the without denies it the possibility of attaining the fulfillment of its desire. But, . . how it does long for color, for sunshine! How its heart yearns for grace, for beauty! How desperately it pleads within itself for freedom from its bondage! The cold, relentless earth denies it all these things . . so it turns away from earth! This is the first step toward its ascent and makes possible its unfoldment.

Can you not see that opposition which drives you in the right direction is good? During the experience it may not be pleasant, but that force which compels expression is a friend, and when you "agree" with it, you will hasten toward your good. All suppression, all deprivation that compels you to listen to the prophet's voice within your soul and urges you into fearless and free expression is a blessing to you. Though it seems to be your enemy, it really is your friend.

Word, thought, idea and Spirit-power bear exactly the same relation to each other that the key, hammer, string and vibration bear to each other in a piano. The vibration, or power within the string is released as sound to the ear only as the key in connection with it is struck. The key C moves the hammer C which touches the string C and releases the vibration C.

In no other way can that particular tone be brought forth. If we want the tone C, we must be particular to strike the key C. In the same way, the word health moves the thought health, and awakens the idea health until the vibration or feeling of health is released in consciousness. It is for this reason that the weak are told to say "I AM strong." Strength is what the weak wish to experience, therefore they must say it and think it and in exact fulfillment of the law of Faith they will feel it, but they will not do so as long as they persist in saying "weak."

These true words, or words declaring the truth of Being, are the "keys of the kingdom" to which Jesus referred when he told Peter, the man of Faith, that they would be given to him. They are given to every Faithful soul who will lift the consciousness above the testimony of the senses, or the opinions of others, and voice the Truth from the prompting of the Spirit within. In no other way can the ' "church" of Christ which is the "temple of the body" be built, for it must be formed from within, but can be only as the word which calls it forth is spoken from without. The kingdom of heaven is within, and the keys which unlock this kingdom to the consciousness of man are the good words or words of God (consciousness) which we speak. We must speak the words that are true of Being, then will the true become manifest, and the false will pass away.

It can be readily seen that when in man lies all power to express, and all substance with which to express, and all intelligence with which to think what form shall be expressed, there remains but one thing necessary to bring forth expression, and that is to decide what form shall be thought into expression, or to intelligently conceive what the power and substance of Being shall produce. This definite decision as to what shall be expressed is like choosing a seed for sun and earth to bring forth. They are willing to produce any harvest man desires, but he himself must decide what he wishes to sow. Even so, power and substance lie within the being of man and will bring forth into expression that which he conceives, or prophesies, if he will only fulfill the law of mind, which is the law of Faith, by "Asking" for what he wants and by believing he has that for which he asks.

Faith is the hidden secret to all the higher powers; therefore, when we enter Faith we enter the conscious possession of those powers, and may employ them for any purpose that is before us now. As we grow in Faith the finer creative energies increase in power, because the more Faith we have the more power we receive from within; we thereby promote the development of talent, genius and rare ability on an ever-increasing scale.

The Subconscious Mind is the agent in changing the polarity of Faith. First, you break up the negative habits of thought into which the Subconscious has drifted by cleansing, by discipline, and by reversal. Then you condition it to hold the positive idea so firmly that it becomes the ruling factor in your thoughts, acts, and words. This can be done in meditation and in the Silence by impressing the idea with deep feeling upon the Subconscious Mind, not spasmodically but consistently. You can accelerate the process by repeating the idea to yourself silently or aloud even as you go about your daily tasks: "My Faith is in God, (consciousness) Omnipotent Good, as the only Presence and the only Power in me and in my affairs." As you do this, the old habit of thought will drop away and the new concept will take its place.

Faith does not simply believe; Faith knows; real Faith is a superior understanding, and deals with tangible facts on all planes. It is not the function of Faith to blindly accept, but to give man the wisdom, and the power to do greater things. Real Faith goes to work, but asks no questions about results. Faith knows that all is possible now, and acts accordingly. Faith enters the larger life and takes up the greater undertakings as if there were no obstacles, and discovers that obstacles cannot exist anywhere.

There can be no expression or growth without Faith, for growth is pressing forth from that which now is into that which is to be expressed. It is making the unseen seen. Not having yet experienced the unseen, we cannot reason about it with conscious knowledge. We must press forth into this new state in Faith, else we can never attain it. Faith is the evidence of things not seen, the substance of things hoped for.

This conscious reaching out, this belief in the unseen, is the evidence that it can be, and this mental quality is in itself the substance of the thing. It is that which underlies the thing hoped for. Faith is the spiritual substance of the thing you desire. It is the invisible side of the visible substance. It is the fixed idea in mind which stands for the formed thing in earth. The image takes form in mind, and becomes form in earth. A thing is first idealized in Faith, and then realized in experience. This is the true materialization.

A Faith That Knows

To fully define this Faith is an effort that will never be attempted, because true Faith is far beyond the description of words; the true Faith is something that must be spiritually discerned, and the higher one ascends in the understanding of the spirit the larger and more powerful this Faith becomes.

Since all is Spirit, then all form must take form in Spirit, the invisible substance, in order to be visible. The idea is perceived in Spirit, it is outlined, or "framed" by the word which gives it form. Through the faculty of Faith this idea is held in mind until it is made firm, enduring, substantial. Becoming substantial, it is materialized, or becomes substance.

This is just what Jesus meant when he said:

"Ask," . . speak the word.
"Believe," . . hold the form in mind.
"And ye shall have," . . it will manifest.

As there is no limit to the form our Faith may take, so there is no limit to the form substance may assume in our experience.

For this reason all things are possible and nothing shall be impossible unto you. "What things soever ye desire, when ye pray, believe that ye receive them, and ye shall have them." There is no limitation except to the mind that fails to grasp this conception of Faith and neglects to give desire definite form, without which it cannot materialize. No flower ever blooms that does not have in its heart the form it is to be. A wise architect has a plan for his house, and the Infinite who is so ready and willing to satisfy the desire of every living creature asks but one thing, . . "What shall I give unto thee? What do you want?"

The type of thought we entertain both creates and draws conditions that crystallize about it, conditions exactly the same in nature as is the thought that gives them form. Thoughts are forces, and each creates of its kind, whether we realize it or not. The great law of the drawing power of the mind, which says that like creates like, and that like attracts like, is continually working in every human life, for it is one of the great immutable laws of the universe. For one to take time to see clearly the things he would attain to, and then to hold that ideal steadily and continually before his mind, never allowing Faith . . his positive thought-forces . . to give way to or to be neutralized by doubts and fears, and then to set about doing each day what his hands find to do, never complaining, but spending the time that he would otherwise spend in complaint in focusing his thought-forces upon the ideal that his mind has built, will sooner or later bring about the full materialization of that for which he sets out.

Two voices are ever whispering to the soul. The one speaks of limitation and impossibility. It is the voice of objective consciousness, that state of mind which sees things as they appear to be. The other speaks of the limitless and reminds the soul that every desire may be fulfilled through Faith. This is the inner prophetic voice of the soul. It is urging a better expression, a complete happiness, a life that is more abundant. Since the within is to be expressed in the without, this is the voice which we must hear if we would know the "land of promise," or experience the good promised to us. It tells us, "Press steadfastly on . . in Faith.

We look out upon life and it seems to us to have little or no meaning. Good and evil forces are struggling for the mastery, but there is no clear evidence that the good is victorious. Yet there is an instinct which tells us that the good ought to win, that the world ought to be a moral world, and that purpose, not chance, should rule. Now the activity of Faith is obedience to this instinct, and the venture of Faith is the impulse within us to make the world what we feel it ought to be, to assume that the true and the good will ultimately be found at one. If we make this assumption and guide our lives by it we shall verify our Faith by the freedom and the expansion and the effectiveness which will be our experience. And so, too, with the pessimistic want of Faith in our fellow-men. This cynical disbelief in the trust-worthiness of human nature can be cast out and kept out only by the deliberate assumption of the opposite. Act as if your fellow-men were worthy of trust, and you will find that in the vast majority of cases your assumption will verify itself. The truth is that our Faith in others has a creative quality. It awakens within men desires, ambitions, dreams of which they had never suspected themselves capable. We are encouraged to exercise this Faith by the example of those who have by their Faith moved humanity to higher issues. All great leaders of men have trusted those whom they led.

The Master made it very clear that healing is accomplished through Faith. It could not be otherwise, for health springs from within. Life which is health must have its source in God (consciousness), the giver of life, who is ever within the soul yearning to quicken soul, mind, body and affairs with power and perfection, but who cannot do so until the principle for this quickening, or outpouring is fulfilled. God (consciousness) is brought forth into expression through the law of Faith and it was for this reason that the Master invariably told those whom he had been able to heal, "Thy Faith hath made thee whole. Thy Faith hath saved thee." Sometimes, before speaking the healing word, he asked the one desiring help, "Believe ye that I AM able to do this?"

When we realize that the larger, the greater and the superior is to be found in the within on a higher plane, and that to gain possession of the superior we must develop the consciousness of the within; that is, consciousness must be expanded to such an extent that it reaches into the within and comprehends the within as well as the without. Since Faith is the only path to the within, and since it is only through Faith that consciousness can be expanded, Faith therefore becomes indispensable to all forms of development. Faith is the hidden secret to the true, the perfect and the limitless in everything; therefore, to find Faith is to find everything. Nothing is hidden from him who has Faith, because he who enters into Faith enters into that which was hidden, and it is hidden no more.

We fear the unknown; but half our fear has vanished when the unknown has been forced to give up its secret. But if a genuinely regenerative force is to enter the life and make peace and poise a permanent possession, something more is needed. Faith in the goodness of life, in the creative spirit of the universe, in the honor of men and in the virtue of women, in the powers of the human soul, and, if by the grace of Heaven we can attain to it, Faith in a destiny rich in boundless possibility is the sovereign cure for this saddest distemper of the soul. No crisis is too great, no agony is too poignant, no upheaval of the foundations of existence too overwhelming for the constraining, steadying, and uplifting energies of a moral trust.

One sometimes imagines oneself in a situation of terrible strain and stress, amid the terrors of shipwreck, or in the inferno of the modem battlefield, where the relentless forces of nature or the cruel engines of human ingenuity make havoc of youth, affection, beauty, the rich promise of the future as well as the garnered harvests of the past, and the doubt arises unbidden . . what would Faith in the invisible order of realities avail against the overpowering might of the immediate present? It suffices us to reply that Faith is not merely for the sunshine, but also for the darkness; not only for the quiet levels of our existence, but also for the wrack of tempest and the last delirium of despair.

There is something in man that is more than human; something that is far greater than the personal man; something that transcends every form of visible existence; something that is created in the image of the Supreme; and it is Faith that unfolds this higher being, causing the Word to become flesh, thereby permeating the visible form with the beauty and the divinity of the soul. It is the nature of Faith to enter the higher, the larger and the boundless; therefore, by living in Faith you will mentally dwell in a growing consciousness of superiority. This will develop superiority in all your talents and faculties, because whatever we become conscious of, that we express through our own mind and character.

Start now to believe, not with the wavering confidence based on deceptive external evidence but with an undaunted confidence based on the immutable law that you can be that which you desire to be. You will find that you are not a victim of fate but a victim of Faith (your own).

Expectation is Faith in action. Expectation is the feeling of fulfillment that comes from conviction. When you ask God (consciousness) for something, you must expect to receive what you ask. Expectation that comes from conviction does not run around beating the air in anxiety and suspense like the bettor at the race track. Expectation is calm, tranquil and confident. Knowing that the desire is already fulfilled, it is quiet, serene and undisturbed. The Expectation that gets phenomenal results wastes no time in speculation or doubt but accepts the promises of God (consciousness) as real and true. The greater your Expectation, the harder your Faith will work and the more it will accomplish. Expect the best, and you will get the best. Expect your Faith to work, and it will work. Expectation is not only a great stimulus to action but is also the push and motive power behind Faith. It causes your Faith to move with greater rapidity and power toward the fulfillment of your desire. Have you decided what you want? Then charge your Mind with tremendous Faith, interest and expectation. Know that your Faith will produce it. Let your feeling of expectation be full, deep, and continuous.

An understanding Faith functions from Principle. It is based on knowledge of Truth. It understands the law of mind action. Therefore, it has great strength. To know that certain causes produce certain results gives a bedrock foundation for Faith.

When we have great and difficult undertakings before us, we should remain calm, and permit supreme power to enter our thoughts; difficulties will instantaneously disappear, the work will almost do itself, and the goal in view will be reached with as perfect ease as the simplest task we ever performed. The great achievement will be the result of higher power; not a power coming to us from some separate, outside source, but a higher power all our own . . our own unbounded power, awakened from the limitless within. Experience teaches that it is neither strenuous nor laborious thinking that produces the greatest results in life, but those high, strong thoughts we create while we are in the secret places . . in the peace that passeth understanding. The hidden path to these secret places is Faith; to enter Faith is to enter the life of higher power, supreme power, limitless power; to enter Faith is to enter the very soul of existence and gain possession of that something that produces all the worth, all the goodness and all the beauty of eternal life; to enter Faith is to enter that rare and wonderful something that is prepared for them that love Him.

Start now to practice what the Bible calls repentance, which is a radical change of attitude. No matter what it is, if it does not conform to your ideal change it by subjectively appropriating your goal. Remain Faithful to it and no earthly power can keep you from attaining it.

The very thought of abundance lifts the mind far beyond the bounds of limitation. One cannot think abundance and conceive things in particular at the same time. It is too large a word to permit of detail. With it in mind, consciousness must swing far out with full sweep into universal existence, and soar unhampered, unbound in the joyousness of perfect freedom.

Consciousness does not attain unto this in a moment. The actual breaking of the last vestige of limitation may be accomplished in an instant, but there is a preparation for the glorious event, . . a preparation in minutest detail . . even as every petal of a poppy is perfected in minutest detail within the confines of its bud, . . but once perfected, the sepals open wide through the force of a last impelling inner urge, and the bloom unfolds, . . gloriously, beautifully free. A moment before its birth it was a prisoner, bound within the sepal sense of self, but an inner perfecting wrought through hourly preparation, grew mightier than the limitation and proved that the limitless, the boundless, awaited a complete readiness to receive it.

Thus it is in the Faith that brings abundance. Like the land of Canaan, the promised abundance awaits the one who has the strength and courage and Faith to enter in. Egyptian bondage must be forsaken, the uncertainties of the wilderness must be overcome, and Canaan must be entered into, . . then only is Canaan gained. On the way to abundance, certain things must be abandoned; tests of Faith are to be met and victories won; new realizations are to be accepted in order that they may be enjoyed. No freedom was ever gained wherein these three steps were not taken, . . decision against the old, adherence to Faith in the new, even while it is as yet unseen, and complete and full acceptance of the new when it is revealed.

Faith is the foundation of all that man does. It is closely related to the enduring, firm, unyielding forms of substance. The development of it is a key to spiritual realization. Faith in God (consciousness) is the substance of existence. To have Faith in God consciousness) is to have the Faith of God (consciousness). We must have Faith in God (consciousness) as our Father and source of all the good we desire.

He who lives constantly in the attitude of Faith will, before long, develop remarkable intellectual brilliancy. He who lives in Faith will not only increase his ability, and the power that does things, but will also acquire that rare and most excellent faculty of doing the right thing at the right time. Faith does develop higher mental insight, thus giving mind the power to act with real wisdom, keen judgment and superior understanding.

The sincere desire made active and accompanied by Faith sooner or later gives place to realization; for Faith is an invisible and invincible magnet, and attracts to itself whatever it fervently desires and calmly and persistently expects. This is absolute, and the results will be absolute in exact proportion as this operation of the thought forces, as this Faith is absolute, and relative in exact proportion as it is relative.

To enter Faith is to enter the life of the limitless power that is within us and all about us; to have Faith . . real Faith, is to open the mind to the influx of that power from within that can do all things; therefore, to have Faith . . the deep, strong, soul Faith, is to reduce failures to nothing. This is another great truth that should be proclaimed from every housetop, and re-echoed throughout the world. Have Faith, and whatever you may undertake to do, that you shall surely accomplish. Limitless power cannot fail, and Faith opens the mind to that power. This proves conclusively that Faith is the hidden secret . . the very secret of all secrets. Faith has the secret, therefore it pays no attention to appearances nor external indications; Faith works upon the principle that whatever we have the desire to accomplish, that we have the power to accomplish; Faith works upon this principle because it knows that there is unbounded power in man; and Faith also knows that man can gain conscious possession of this power by having Faith in Faith.

Consider the respective activities of fear and Faith. Fear disintegrates, Faith unifies; fear weakens, Faith invigorates; fear depresses, Faith exalts; fear inhibits, Faith sets free. In brief, fear lowers our vitality, lessens the sum total of our muscular, moral, and intellectual energies. What we need is not more knowledge, but more trust.

As it takes Faith to leave the old state of material bondage wherein we receive only that which the law of sense determines for us, and again an increase of Faith to meet the tests that compel us to rely upon the unseen power to provide for the daily needs, still again it requires Faith in an intensified degree to know I AM, supply, . . that where I AM God (consciousness) is, and where God (consciousness) is, all is. Therefore, abundance is here where I am, for I AM the boundless, limitless abundance of power, substance and intelligence of God (consciousness), present in all places, under all circumstances and at all times. This is the promised land, the fulfillment of Faith that admits of no limitation, that recognizes no lack, that abides in the consciousness of abundance and hence lives and loves and gives. It is the exercising of Faith that "worketh by love," for love is the fulfilling of the law, . . the perfecting of it.

Faith is nothing more nor less than the operation of the thought-forces in the form of an earnest desire, coupled with expectation as to its fulfillment. And in the degree that Faith, the earnest desire thus sent out, is continually held to and watered by firm expectation, in just that degree does it either draw to itself, or does it change from the unseen into the visible, from the spiritual into the material, that for which it is sent.

In reality miracles are events that take place as a result of the operation of a higher, unknown law. All true action is governed by law. Nothing just happens. All happenings are the result of cause and can be explained under the law of cause and effect. Mighty things have been wrought in the past by those who had mere blind Faith to guide them. To Faith we now add understanding of the law.

The universal can supply all things; therefore, he who lives constantly in perfect touch with the universal will never want for anything. When you have Faith in yourself you awaken the immensity of your own interior life, and bring into expression your better self, your superior self, your limitless self.

WHAT HAPPENS TO FAITH THAT IS NOT USED?

The same thing that happens to the tires on an automobile that is not used. To keep the rubber flexible and resilient, the car must be used. So it is with Faith. Faith if not used, it becomes static and weak. It is like a pool of water that is not agitated; it lacks power. Just as our muscles develop through exercise, Faith grows through use. The Law says, "Use or lose."

Have Faith in your work, and your efforts will produce far greater results; because through the attitude of Faith you give your very best life and power to your work. In addition you enter into a more perfect harmony with all the elements contained in your work, thereby producing that unity of purpose which invariably culminates in great achievements. Have Faith in every opportunity and the richest treasures that may be hidden within that opportunity will be given to you. Faith enters the soul of things and gains possession of the very essence of all worth. Wherever there is a secret, Faith will find it. Have Faith in every circumstance, in every phase of environment and these will give only their best to you. When you have Faith, adverse environments will trouble you no more; they will, on the other hand, become open gates to pastures green. Nothing but the best can come through Faith, therefore it is the hidden secret to the best that anything in the world can give.

You can think of your life as mental; every faculty will begin to buzz with new life. Your life will never wane if you keep in the consciousness of it as Mind or Spirit; it will increase and attain full expression in your body. If you have Faith in the life idea in your consciousness, your body will never be run down but will become more and more alive with spiritual life.

It is the substance of things hoped for, even as Paul declared. Faith is beyond hope, for things "hoped for" are formed, actually made of, the substance of Faith. Hope is mere yearning, and but creates the desire which opens the way to the fullness of Faith. Faith is the understanding that gives fixity to the consciousness. It does not waver. A wavering Faith is no Faith at all. It is doubt and unbelief. Only the Faith that is fixed, or substantial, can be the substance of things hoped for.

By having Faith in yourself you bring to the surface the best that you possess, and then proceed to gain conscious possession of better talents and greater powers than you have ever known before. There is a genius asleep in the subconscious of every mind; in the great within of every mind, unbounded capacity and ability may be found; and it is Faith that awakens this genius; it is Faith that unfolds the limitless possibilities within. Faith is the hidden secret to greatness, because Faith takes man into the inner life of that power that produces greatness. Therefore, he who has Faith in himself may become anything, attain anything and accomplish anything. To have Faith in yourself is to feel the life and power of that something within yourself that is limitless; that something that is created in the image and likeness of the Supreme.

Faith is the hidden secret to all supply, and he who enters Faith, by having Faith in Faith, will find the world of limitless supply. To the mind of mere reason this may not seem true, but it is true; Faith knows it to be true, and the light of Faith is higher than the light of reason. It is, therefore, well in the beginning, not to reason too much about the why's and the wherefore's of Faith. To reason about that which the outer mind cannot understand will confuse consciousness and prevent that serene state of perfect assurance which is necessary to Faith. Know that Faith can do everything: and know that Faith will reveal to you exactly how it is done; then have more Faith; before long, Faith will become so strong that even reason will be convinced, and will cooperate with Faith in demonstrating to the outer mind that the claims of Faith are true . . absolutely true.

Not only does it take Faith to disregard the appearance and call forth the ideal, but it takes a continuance of Faith to establish the ideal in consciousness and make it real in experience. The word we speak is but a seed. Like every seed it grows first beneath the soil, hidden from view. When the seed-word is spoken it takes root in the soil of the mind. It will surely bring forth after its kind, and we will "reap in due time, . . if we faint not."

When things seem to go wrong, do not complain about the incompetence of man, but have Faith in man, and the better side of everybody with which you are connected, will appear to set all matters right. The complaining mind goes down into more confusion and denser mental darkness, thereby making more mistakes and misleading everybody concerned to a lesser or greater extent. It is the truth that the more we complain the more we shall find about which to complain; and the more we contend with things the more things we shall have with which to contend.

IS IT TRUE THAT NEGATIVE THOUGHT ACTS WITH GREATER POWER AND RAPIDITY THAN POSITIVE THOUGHT?

No, it is not; it only seems that way. The force of any thought whether negative or positive is always in direct ratio to our Faith. If we have more Faith in evil than in good, the results will be more negative than positive.

The bringing forth of Spirit substance into definite form is accomplished through definite law, and until this law is fulfilled there can be no demonstration. Spirit forms according to the conception held in mind through Faith. For this reason all things are to us according to our Faith. Until Faith in the thing desired is established in the mind, it cannot assume definite form in the experience, and the reason that so many undesirable things take form in our lives is because, unconsciously, we have held in mind, or have had Faith in, a conception which we really dreaded to experience. The mind must be trained to hold only ideal, truthful conceptions in order that ideal and truthful expression may be made manifest.

Faith ignores all the limitations of objective intelligence and enters the larger mental world of superior intelligence; Faith knows that the dark unknown will be found to be filled with light after we have entered its luminous splendor, and by entering this more brilliant mental world, Faith proves that its Faith was true.

To live in Faith is to live a larger and a greater life perpetually, because it is the nature of Faith to enlarge, expand and develop everything that pertains to the mental and spiritual life.

To desire, with the whole heart and soul, what we need or wish for, and to place unbounded Faith in that desire, will in every instance produce results. This principle can be applied to everything on all planes of life; there is therefore, no reason why anyone should ever want for anything.

The greatest power that can be expressed through the mind of man comes from the united actions of desire and Faith. This power is actually irresistible; therefore, whatever we desire in Faith, that we shall positively receive. Have Faith, and no true desire shall remain unfulfilled; not that we shall always receive the very identical thing desired, because that would frequently prove undesirable; but the desire will be fulfilled. When we do not receive the very thing desired we shall receive something that will serve our purpose far better.

With the objective senses tightly shut you can make the insensibly felt (the subjective state) seem real or sensibly known, for Faith is knowledge.

Since thought starts every creation and is backed up by all the mind and all the power there is, can your thought lack creative force? IT CANNOT! Declare this truth: "I have Faith in Faith. I have Faith in myself. I have Faith in creative activity. I have Faith in the outcome of my own Faith. I AM full of quiet confidence. I AM calm. I AM serene. I AM confident. 'Thou wilt keep him in perfect peace whose mind is stayed on Thee.'"

Faith can do all things because it uses all things and works in harmony with all things. Faith enters into the very life of life, and is therefore in the soul of life; to be in the soul of life is to feel, realize and receive the life that contains all power, all wisdom and all love. Through Faith man can do all things, because Faith awakens that something in man that can do all things.

Think of the power given to man through Faith, "Nothing shall be impossible unto you!" What more could be promised? What could be more all inclusive? Not one condition of limitation is suggested except the limitation which one gives to his own Faith.

The powers that create, the forces that build, the elements that promote the growth of mind and soul . . all of these come from the same inner source, and will come in greater abundance as the inner world is awakened in the mind of man. The love that loves everything with real love also comes from the wonderful within; likewise, purity, virtue, kindness, harmony, joy and the peace that passeth understanding. All of these may be obtained in boundless supply through the living of life in Faith.

Faith is the fire of Spirit. Faith opens the door into an inner consciousness, where we hold the word steadily in mind until the spiritual substance responds to our word. Earnest, steady, and continued attention along this line is bound to bring forth the fruits of the Spirit in abundant measure. A steady, unwavering devotion of heart to the Spirit develops in us supermind qualities.

That we must have Faith before we can become conscious of the new, the larger, the better, the higher, the spirit of things, is very evident when we realize that it is Faith alone that goes out upon the seeming void; it is Faith alone that breaks bounds and demonstrates the existence of a greater life; it is Faith that takes the first step forward always, but wherever Faith may go, consciousness invariably follows.

It is important in acquiring Faith, to learn first of all to value the need that inspires Faith to action. Instead of feeling alarm at the need which is present in your life, see it as prepared ground that calls for a seed. This need demands satisfaction. It is there to compel you to conceive that which will fulfill the need. When you have once named it you have conceived an idea which if held Faithfully (or perfectly imaged in your mind in Faith) will be given birth in your experience. Blessed is the emptiness that arouses your consciousness to the point of conceiving that which will fill it.

The man who has Faith in everybody will never have much to complain about; the best of everything will come with him into his way, and all things will work together for his good. There is nothing that will smoothen the pathway of life, and harmonize all the conditions of life more perfectly and more rapidly than a full, strong, living Faith . . a Faith that has Faith in everybody and in everything. When we have Faith in everything we are brought into closer touch with the best of everything, and will thus secure the best from every source.

Faith will move in any direction Mind gives it. Faith will accomplish anything Mind decrees. Faith will do anything that Mind directs. When Faith is directed toward God (consciousness), man gains access to unlimited power. Working with Principle, Faith knows how to build a successful business. Faith knows how to turn ideas into cash. Faith knows how to take a sick body and make it well. Faith knows how to take a failure and turn it into a success. Faith does not have to argue or reason. Faith knows and knows that it knows. There is no limit to the power of the Principle of Faith. Faith will take a man to where he wants to be or leave "Him" where he is. The only limiting factor is unbelief.

Faith is feeling, "According to your Faith (feeling) be it unto you." You never attract that which you want but always that which you are. As a man is, so does he see. "To him that hath it shall be given and to him that hath not it shall be taken away..." That which you feel yourself to be you are, and you are given that which you are. So assume the feeling that would be yours were you already in possession of your wish, and your wish must be realized. You are that which you believe yourself to be.

Be still, and know that you are in the presence of a power that is supreme, a power that can do all things, and every thought you think will contain this power, and will do with this power whatever your heart may desire to have done. To secure more power do not try to force the power you may already possess, but enter those higher spiritual realms, through Faith, where power is limitless; and when you enter that state your thoughts not only become enormously strong, but thinking becomes so smooth and so gentle that you think the most wonderful thoughts and the most powerful thoughts, even without any effort whatever.

SEE YOURSELF AS SPIRIT

A good method is to image the body as pure spirit, to see yourself as spirit living in a world of spirit, unhampered by grosser forms called matter. Dream yourself as existing in this pure world of spirit. You are thus seeing yourself ideally. You are seeing yourself as you are in the potential power of being. Then the creative life within you takes this idea of itself and begins to construct accordingly. So you find that "you do not have to struggle; you only have to know." Let no one fasten upon you the thought that your trouble is incurable. Who is he that shall usurp your rights of image-formation? Who shall supplant your picture-forming power? Shall you accept his dictum? The language of creative activity is visualization, the articulation of vision is thought, the expression of thought is objective realization. Creation never ceases. Therefore do not despair before the verdict of the physician. You are the metaphysician. You are the master within the temple of your body. Have Faith, only believe, and "it shall be done unto you of my Father."

To enter Faith, turn mind upon the inner side of life, and mentally dwell upon the inner reality that permeates all things. This reality may be termed a shining reality because it is the very essence of light, purity and perfection. When you are in Faith your mind actually enters into this essence, and thereby awakens the unbounded life that absolute reality contains It is for this reason that Faith can see you through anything; no matter what your obstacles or difficulties may be, simply have Faith; Faith will see you through. Live in the Faith that everything is coming the way you desire, and as your Faith is, so shall it be.

When mind is in the attitude of Faith there is no fear of adversity; there is not even any thought of adversity, because while in Faith the mind is above all adverseness; it is in peace, harmony and rightness; it is in the life of that power that can, and does cause everything to move smoothly, and all things to work together for good. While in Faith the mind has no fear of failure; Faith never thinks of failure; Faith sees the possibilities of success; Faith knows that success in every instance is possible because it knows that all things are possible; Faith does not ask if success will come, but opens the mind to the great power within that positively will produce success.

It is Faith that fills the soul with that strange determination that carries you on and on through all sorts of conditions, and finally brings you to the very mountaintop of attainment and achievement.

Even if you do not see all the way through your Faith, you still have a right to believe that you are justified in believing.

Faith is the hidden secret to every desire and need of man; therefore, all things are possible to him who has Faith; and all things desired shall come to him who lives, thinks and acts in the very soul of that Faith that is Faith.

If Faith in a mind with no native religious tendency can enable it to face with courage and resolution the worst that fate can do, are we not justified in saying that we are in the presence of the greatest power known to humanity?

When you have brought into experience the fulfillment of a heart's desire through the definite law of Faith you will value the law. It will be more wonderful to you than the fulfillment of your desire. When you have proved God's law (the law of consciousness), you will love God (consciousness), and praise Him for the means He has given you through which you may establish perfect freedom in all your affairs. You will rejoice because the law of the Lord is perfect. It will convert your soul. That is, it will fire your soul with a great appreciation of this "treasure in heaven," or law of mind, which you must seek "first" in order to have the "added thing," because it is this law which forms the added thing, or makes it possible.

What you do not understand leave to Faith; Faith is the hidden secret to all understanding, and by having Faith in Faith, the secret of everything will be revealed to you. Since Faith is the hidden secret, to enter into Faith is to enter into this same secret; henceforth, nothing will be hidden from you. To him who lives in Faith there are no problems; life is clear, the purpose of life is clear, the law of living the life is clear, the path to endless ascension in life is clear . . everything is clear; and it is also clear that all things will be according to the measure of Faith.

You do not have to change your occupation to introduce Faith into practical life; if your occupation is legitimate, remain where you are; use the methods you have used before, no matter how material they may seem to be; make no startling changes in the without; meet the world in the usual way, and deal with the world in a way that the world can understand, knowing that all things are good that are turned to good account; but make this change . . give your occupation soul by working in Faith.

The Master said, "What things soever ye desire, when ye pray, believe that ye receive them and ye shall have them." Can any law be more clearly enunciated, can anything be more definite and more absolute than this? According to thy Faith be it unto thee. Do we at times fail in obtaining the results we desire? The fault, the failure, lies not in the law but in ourselves. Regarded in its right and true light, than prayer there is nothing more scientific, nothing more valuable, nothing more effective.

Faith gives invincible power to everything; Faith is the hidden secret to all power; therefore, to enter Faith is to enter the secret of Faith, and the secret is hidden from you no more; the great within is opened before you, and unlimited power is at your command.

It is a mental law that any idea held firmly in the Mind expresses itself in the body and affairs. But the only ideas that can be held firmly in the Mind are those in which we have Faith. The purpose of concentration in Faith is to direct all our thoughts, feelings, and activities toward the fulfillment of our desire; in other words, to pinpoint the desire until it has been realized.

As man comes into the presence of God (consciousness) with his prayer in the form of an affirmation of Truth, holding the prayer steadily in mind and consciously unifying his mind with the mind of God (consciousness), he is aware only of the soundlessness of God's (consciousness) Word as it weaves itself in and out through the whole soul and body consciousness, illumining, redeeming, and restoring him according to his Faith and trust, according to his strength and power to receive.

When you have found your work, have Faith, and press on. Do not stop to wonder if you are to succeed; have the Faith that you will succeed, and nothing in the world can prevent you from reaching the very highest goal you may have in view.

Cleanse your thought of the sense of lack. God (consciousness) being all, he cannot be more or less, hence has no thought of gain or of loss. Whether his Being is expressed or unexpressed, still he is being God (consciousness) . . the whole thing . . the absolute allness of all there is. H2O is H2O whether the form be gas, steam, rain, dew, ice or snow. So is God (consciousness) always God (consciousness) whether in Being, or state (form) of Being. He is to you as you ask him to be, for "Everyone that asketh receiveth."

The industrial world will not be purified by making changes in the without, but by awakening the higher powers from within; the man who enters the industrial world may not expect to reach his goal in view by hard work on the surface, but by permeating his work with limitless power from within. This he may do by having Faith in his work; by thinking of his work as good, not material, and by having such a perfect Faith in Faith that fear concerning results is entirely eliminated from his mind.

Faith is more than mere belief. It is the very substance of that which is believed. Faith working in spiritual substance accomplishes all things. This is the Faith that cooperates with creative law. When it is exercised deep in spiritual consciousness, it finds its abode. Here it works under divine law, without variation. It brings results that are seemingly miraculous.

To try to become conscious of something that is beyond the present capacity of consciousness, produces a shock to the mind; a fact that everyone knows who has tried to comprehend the universe with the limitations of the personal mind; but when the mind works and thinks in Faith, consciousness expands constantly, naturally and of its own accord, thus producing perpetual and normal growth of mind.

Just as a seed must be established in the earth before it will start to grow, so must an idea be established in mind before it will begin to express. A wavering mind is not established, and James tells us that in this consciousness we can never hope to receive from the Lord or from the outworking of the law. "Let him ask in Faith, nothing wavering. For he that wavereth is like a wave of the sea, driven with the wind and tossed, for let not that man think he shall receive anything of the Lord"

To have Faith in Faith is to open the mind to an inner world of sublime existence . . a life of indescribable beauty and unfathomable joy. It is this life of which we gain occasional glimpses while we are on the mountain top of spiritual thought; and it is in these states that we behold that something that tongue can never picture nor the mind of man understand.

"**Now do I have that serene consciousness** that is sure of the fact that thought controls substance and passes it out into form. Now do I feel, deep within my being, that the things I desire shall come to pass. I riot only know that these things can be but that they will be. I am conscious of the fact that I and the Father are one. He is creative; I AM creative: He is changeless substance; I AM changeless substance: He is eternal; I AM eternal: He is perfect; I AM perfect: He is complete; I AM complete. As He creates by thinking, so do I. I AM conscious of myself as self directing. I have Faith; I believe in the power of my own word to bring things forth out of the invisible."

Faith is the evidence of things not seen, because Faith does see what has not been seen; Faith knows that the unseen is real and substantial; Faith proves that the unseen can be seen by those who will awaken the superior mind within; therefore, by entering into Faith we enter into the realization of the real and see all things as they are in the perfect state.

Faith is a quality of consciousness which gives evidence of its use through the effects its produces. Faith which does not manifest in works is not Faith, but doubt and unbelief. Thus, in endeavoring to acquire Faith, we are not seeking a blind belief in an intangible, impractical, mystical something which lies ever beyond us, but are seeking to ascertain the way to use a force which operates according to a definite law, and produces definite results.

Faith proves that the great unknown is unknown only to those who have not begun to live the larger life; but to follow Faith is to enter the new life, because Faith goes on and reveals the wonders and the powers of the larger spheres of existence; not simply those spheres that may exist beyond the scope of sense, but also those spheres that exist all about us, here and now, within the very world of sense.

Nothing is more subtle than thought, nothing more powerful, nothing more irresistible in its operations, when rightly applied and held to with a Faith and fidelity that is unswerving, . . a Faith and fidelity that never knows the neutralizing effects of doubt and fear. If one have aspirations and a sincere desire for a higher and better condition, so far as advantages, facilities, associates, or any surroundings or environments are concerned, and if he continually send out his highest thought forces for the realization of these desires, and continually water these forces with firm expectation as to their fulfillment, he will sooner or later find himself in the realization of these desires, and all in accordance with natural laws and forces.

WHY MUST THE DESIRE BE FREED BEFORE IT CAN BE FULFILLED?

You might as well ask why the seed must be dropped into the ground before it can bring the increase. Seed cannot grow in your hand, on the shelf, or in the packet. Nor can your desire materialize if you hold it tightly in your thought. Jesus told us to Take no thought in order to give the desire a chance to go forth and bring back its reward. Since the desire cannot be in two places at the same time, we must choose between fulfillment or frustration, between letting-go or holding-on. Jesus says that the seed must be dropped in the ground and that the desire must be relinquished to God (consciousness). Take no thought does not mean lapsing into a state of unconsciousness; it means taking away the anxiety and fear which prevent the manifestation of your desire. When you release the desire in absolute forgetfulness, as Jesus did, the reward will come flowing into you in limitless measure. The way of fulfillment is not through thought but through God (consciousness).

We have done well when we have decided against limitation; we have done better when through persistent practice of Faith we have proved the power of the law to demonstrate that Spirit will indeed form as supply from day to day to meet every particular need, but we have done best, when we have passed beyond the proving of the presence of supply for particular needs, and have entered the land "o'er flowing with milk and honey," . . have so completely entered into the promise of Faith that we take "no thought" as to what we shall eat or what we shall wear, but find ourselves living in supply itself since in God (consciousness) himself, and therefore in abundance.

If you were the host at a banquet and had provided an abundant supply of good and desirable things for the pleasure of your guests, would it not be your wish to serve them as they desired? Would you take offense because they might choose one thing and not another? Certainly not. You would desire only that they should state their request. Your pleasure would be in fulfilling it. Can you not understand, then, the consciousness of the all-bountiful and beautiful God (consciousness) of whom the Master says, "Will he not give good things to them that ask him?" Therefore, ask God (consciousness). Ask for what you do want, and do not name, or outline, to the ever-responsive Spirit that which you do not want. For every idle word that you speak you shall be required to give an account thereof in the day of judgment, or at that time when the word you have "framed" takes form in your experience.

The greatest freedom will come to your mind when you realize that Faith is a law, and that it is a law for the use of every one. Just as the principle of mathematics may be used by all, so may the law of Faith be used. Many apply this law unconsciously and create for themselves desirable conditions which many of the "children of the light" fail to enjoy because they fear to use the very law which the Spirit has given man in order that he may exercise his "dominion in earth." The law of Faith is the law that brings freedom. Paul says, "Before Faith came, we were under the law . . . but after that Faith is come we are no longer under a schoolmaster." In other words, after Faith is revealed to us as a law, we ourselves become masters and use it. The Master Jesus was astonished at our lack of Faith. "How is it that ye have no Faith!" he exclaimed. And again, "O, wherefore didst thou doubt?"

Try to see very clearly that Faith is not hope, neither is it belief. Today you may believe something, and tomorrow, something else. Your belief may be strengthened into hope, but even your hope will not demonstrate for you. It but leads to the Faith that creates. Hope is like a bottomless bucket. As fast as water is dipped in a bottomless bucket, it runs out. That is why you may hope and hope and hope, but never receive. Faith puts a bottom in the bucket. What it dips it keeps. It holds the substance, gives it definite form, and establishes the thing you desire. "Faith is the substance of things (hoped for" At first, you hope, but at last you have Faith. Then you demonstrate, and not before.

Have Faith, and sorrow, sickness, trouble and misfortune shall vanish completely; all mountains shall be removed, and nothing shall be impossible unto you. Have Faith, and all your desires shall positively be fulfilled; Faith and desire united as One can bring anything, produce anything, create anything, and cause anything to transpire in the life of man.

Whatever we may require for attainment, advancement, or the enlargement of life, we may secure from the great within; and since Faith is the royal path to this marvelous realm, we understand again why all things are possible to him who has Faith.

The average individual, not knowing the truth, holds fear in the hour of need instead of Faith, and creates a fearful image in mind, thus increasing the difficulty. "Fear not," said the Master. "Have Faith, and doubt not." This seems easy to say, but you inquire, "How can I avoid the doubt amid such trying circumstances?" Here the soul needs to be strengthened by the example of others who have proved the way through Faith. Paul makes this clear in his words, "Now Faith cometh by hearing, but hearing by the word of God (consciousness)." In such an hour of doubt one would do well to read the eleventh chapter of Hebrews, and then make a study of all those mentioned who received a "good report," or had good reported of them, because they acted in Faith, not seeing the way, but believing in the operation of a law which is beyond sight, and which never fails to produce results for the Faithful.

There are many, however, who cannot receive their inspiration from reading stories about those who seem but mystical in character. They demand something more at hand. To these I would say in words of my own, "Now Faith cometh by seeing, by seeing the works of God (consciousness)." The conscious mind cannot see the actual working, for that is done by a mind higher than the conscious mind, but illustrations can be seen to show the law, and so lead the conscious mind to trust, or have Faith in this higher power. Take for instance in the conception of a child. Father and mother conceive the child. That action is of the conscious mind, but beyond this they cannot go. The formation of the child's body is accomplished without their conscious knowledge. This is done for them by a mind beyond the conscious, and indeed if their conscious mind were allowed to act in this matter it would be but an interference.

Even so, in the action of Faith, when the conscious mind with its thinking, its reasoning, its arguments, its questions, attempts to assist, it but interferes and prevents. The conscious mind can do one thing alone and then it must rest. It can ask for what it wants, but then it must have the Faith to believe that the fulfillment of that desire is being formed by a law which works without assistance from the objective plane. The conscious mind can know, and must know, what it wants, then the soul, or higher mind, forms what is wanted. Man in his need asks, God (consciousness) in his fullness gives. Thus the child takes the part of the child, and the Father takes the part of the Father. The Father gives, and the child receives. "Ask and receive, that your joy may be full," said the Master.

This asking in recognition of the higher power must be done in the Faith of a little child, and it is only this childlike state of mind that ever receives the full reward of Faith, for the child is willing to receive, indeed it knows naught but to receive. Its consciousness is open, expectant, receptive, and therefore the fullness can come to it. It is good for the "grown up" consciousness, that which feels itself to be so intellectual, and which knows so much about things (but which has never entered into or become one with the heart of things) to really examine this phase of its consciousness. What does it really know anyway? What can it really know? Spirit and intellect are as widely different as the sun and the moon. The moon has a light about it from the sun, but the sun is light in itself. Therefore, souls must enter more and more into the heart of things, enter into the Spirit of life, and allow the Spirit to play through them as it does through its whole creation. It is the Spirit that holds the vast universe poised in power and perfect form. It is the Spirit that teaches the little birds to build their nests in the Faith that by and by there will be eggs to fill them. It is the Spirit that moves the clouds, turns the wind, holds the sea in its place, paints the glorious sunset, dawns in the sunrise, tints the leaves, colors and unfolds the flowers, gurgles in the brook, plays in the fountain, sings in the heart, frolics through the dear little wild creatures and laughs in innocent happiness through the little child!

How can one live upon the earth and miss seeing the spirit of things? How can one doubt the presence of Spirit and fail to have the Faith to yield to Spirit? Surely, "Faith cometh by seeing, . . by seeing the works of God (consciousness)," as I have said. We need but to open our eyes, and acknowledge that we are one with a unified creation which lives and moves and has its being in the God (consciousness) that lives and moves and expresses his Being through it.

Certainly we are compassed about by this great number of witnesses. Living among them, how can we feel anxious because of tomorrow? How easy it is, if we will but hear their testimony, to "toil not," but rather "to consider the lilies, how they grow." How simple a thing to rest in the promise, "If God (consciousness) so clothe the grass of the field, will he not much more clothe you, oh ye of little Faith?" But see things in their larger sense, but awaken to the fact of a unified creation, but fit yourself into the whole of it, opening to the fullness, the allness of life, and you cannot be Faithless, but Faith full. Once to see this, leaves no room for doubt, for Faith fills the soul to the uttermost.

We exercise Faith when we go to bed at night, for we cannot foretell the events of the morning, and know not what shall occur while we are sleeping, yet we close our eyes in perfect Faith, planning the work of the day to come. In Faith we think and speak and act. Few among us know aught of the power of thought and of the possibilities of construction and destruction that lie in the spoken word, but in thinking and in speaking we ignorantly use Faith, little guessing how the result may react upon us. Few understand the process of the assimilation of food, yet all eat in Faith, and the silent, unseen forces of the mind that are greater than those of the conscious realm, calmly and perfectly do their work. Without knowing how they do it we trust them; we have Faith, and it is done. The farmer plants his grain for the next season's harvest in Faith; He does not understand why or how the little seeds sprout and grow, but without knowing, he does his part in Faith, though perchance he would never think of it as such. When he has done his work, the sun, the earth, the rain, the dew, the air and the very seed he plants, do their part in obedience to laws that his objective mind does not comprehend, yet which Faithfully operate above the plane of his consciousness. It is but another step to deliberately use this Faith for a definite end, still trusting the operation of a law that may be altogether unknown to the outer realm of thought. The Faith we use when we retire is in the dark of night. In times of uncertainty, or in darkened consciousness, we often are obliged to speak and act. It is in the time of hunger that we have the Faith to eat. It is when there is need of a harvest that we sow. Is it then an unnatural thing that in the hour of despair, in a time of direst need, in the midst of a distressing sense of lack, we should still be called upon to exercise Faith in the operation of a law that works beyond the plane of the conscious mind? Indeed it is most natural that this should be so. In Paul's epistles he many times emphasizes the fact that a Faith that is seen is not Faith, and this is indeed true, for Faith is always the "substance of things hoped for" or that quality of the mind that reaches toward the desire of the heart, "as seeing the invisible." There could not be a reaching toward the desire if there were no desire, and there could be no desire if there were no need. Therefore the need awakens the desire. Once outlined in the mind, the desire is first hoped for, then hoped for with such conscious conviction that it becomes real to consciousness. Hope is thus raised to Faith, and Faith is the substance through which the imaged desire becomes an imaged reality, or a real image.

Faith does not dwell apart from things, but works through things, giving to all things an abundance of the unbounded power from within. Without the spirit of Faith, things become lifeless, soulless, purposeless and useless. Everything is limited when Faith is absent; everything breaks bounds when Faith appears.

Fear is negative Faith. Before we can fear anything, we must first have Faith in it. In fact, there can be no fear without Faith. Fear is Faith in evil.

DEMONSTRATING FAITH THROUGH CLAIMING IT

To awaken our own consciousness to larger Faith, we must, therefore, call upon all these resources. And this is as simple as any other demonstration. Simply declare, " I have perfect Faith; and I AM receptive to every thought of true Faith anywhere."

The result of this statement will be to set up a magnet in the mind to attract all the helpful, hopeful, optimistic Faith-thoughts within and without. You have declared that you have Faith. The mind takes that as its picture-model. It begins to collect out of the hidden reservoirs of memory all the Faiths of yesterday. It assembles them in orderly array, prepared to march against the army of your fears and erect the temple of your Faith. Silently the thought, "I have Faith in the power of my word; I have the healing consciousness," begins to take upon it the body of which it is the soul. This word becomes the law of life for your mind, " I have Faith; I AM confident of the success which shall attend my every word." Even as you sleep, the sleepless mind goes on to build your temple, begins to "utter the thoughts that arise in you." As you scan the pages of books and magazines, there come forth to greet your eye the pictures of beautiful deeds and Faith. You do not see the accounts of infidelity, shamefully featured as "news," but only the finer and more glorious acts of men. As you listen to the voices of the multitude, you do not hear jar nor jangle, fear, nor fault; you hear only those who speak words of comfort and who look with even eye of Faith out onto life's landscapes. You become selective of the best because you have declared, "I have Faith." Thus you draw to you thoughts that are inspiring and hopeful. You become a center for the attraction and radiation of Faith. Through the open doors of mind and heart come the songs celestial, "Faith is the victory that overcomes the world."

Thus Faith can be demonstrated, thus you come at last to have the Faith for which you long to make your home in the Heart of the Infinite. Daily declare, "I have this supreme wisdom, this mighty Faith; I AM at one with all Faith; I AM safe in the Infinite Mind of God (consciousness)." And," according to your Faith it shall be done unto you."

To follow Faith is to move forward steadily and surely, even under the most adverse and trying conditions; to follow fear is to go down to failure and defeat even under the most favorable conditions in existence. To banish fear, have Faith; the only infallible remedy for fear is Faith; Faith in all things, and at all times. Faith sees the substance and gains the substance; fear sees the shadow and is soon left with nothing but the shadow.

Desire is the matrix or mold through which Faith works. It is the pattern through which demonstrations are made. Since the Law of Faith is impersonal and works for the bad as well as the good, and since we are continually believing in something, Faith must have a guide. Whatsoever things ye desire when ye pray, believe that ye have received them and ye shall have them. When the desire is drawn out to a point (clearly defined), it becomes a demand. Our claim must be specific. We must have a vivid mental picture of what we want and here the imaginative faculty comes in. If you can imagine it, you can have it.

"Thou shalt love thy neighbor as thyself" This means, that if we are to claim the privilege of bringing forth the divine ideal from within us in perfect freedom, we must of necessity extend the same privilege to our fellow-man. He has the same right to use the law to bring himself forth that we have. Each man must climb his own mountain, receive his own pattern, and bring forth his own ideal. If we fail to accord him this privilege, and in anger condemn him because he fails to worship in our way . . our own ideal crumbles into nothingness, we have broken the whole law, and will have to ascend the mountain again for a more perfect conception of the ideal. When the scribe who listened to this commandment as given by Jesus saw the great reasonableness of this, and exclaimed that it was "more than burnt offerings and sacrifices," the Master replied, "Thou art not far from the kingdom of God (consciousness)."

What depth of meaning in the Master's reply! We are not far from the kingdom of God (consciousness) when we can accept this intellectually as true, but we are in the kingdom, literally of it, when we dare to prove its truth by our acts. Hearing and thinking never take us into the kingdom though they may bring us near to it. Action alone makes the ideal real. The ideal is to be given physical birth. When we do the works then are we being manifest, or manifesting Being, and until Being is made manifest in us we are not in the kingdom of God (consciousness), that is, have not yet brought forth the ideal into actual form. It is doing that builds the house. "He that heareth my word and doeth it," the Master said, builds his house on the rock that winds and waves cannot destroy. Each soul must hear and do for himself. Each soul must climb the mountain peak of illumination for the pattern as God (consciousness) desires it brought forth, then each must descend from the mount prepared to meet his tests and build for himself as he himself has seen. Thus with the love of his heart, soul, mind, and strength centered upon the good . . the perfect ideal, . . the power of God (consciousness) flows out into perfect expression, and God (consciousness) builds the temple of his body, . . a holy temple, indeed, as holy as God (consciousness), himself, has idealized it. It is this "Faith of God (consciousness)" which each must accept for himself in order to demonstrate perfection.

When we have Faith in all things our attention is subconsciously concentrated upon the best; we thereby think the best, create the best, and enter into the world of the best. By entering into the world of the best we shall have the privilege to associate with the best, appropriate the best and live the best. The secret of high thinking and right thinking is therefore found in Faith; and as man is as he thinks we again realize the unbounded value of Faith.

Declare your Faith; and it shall be justified by the fact. "I AM surrounded only by the finest and best people. They are people whom I can trust." No one is going to go back on their word with you; no one is going to deceive you; no one is seeking your injury. You are protected by the inviolability of your own soul. Only these things can reach you to which you are mentally open. So, "Today I AM filled with perfect peace and Faith in everybody and everything. Life is worthwhile for it is under my control; and I can be what I will to be."

Prosperity does not mean the same thing to any two persons. Some people think of prosperity as something separate from their spiritual experience. They live in two worlds. It is not a crime to be rich nor a virtue to be poor. Take God (consciousness) into all your affairs. Do all things to the glory of God (consciousness) seven days a week. Be alert in doing whatever comes to you to do. Be cheerful and competent in the doing, sure of the results. No one is ever given the keys to the Father's storehouse of wealth until he has proved his Faith and his reliability. Supply unfolds at the same rate as the need or ability to use substance is developed. The more conscious you become of the presence of the living substance the more it will manifest itself for you and the richer will be the common good of all. There is an inherent faculty that instinctively lays hold of what it calls its own. The power of the mind to draw to us those things to which we are divinely entitled is a power that can be cultivated, and should be. Substance in the form of money is given to us for constructive uses. It is given for use and to meet an immediate need, not to be hoarded away or be foolishly wasted. If you ask for money, do not look for an angel from the skies to bring it on a golden platter. Keep your eyes open for some fresh opportunity to make money. An opportunity will come as sure as you live. Money is man's instrument, not his master. Money was made for man, not man for money. It is not money that controls men, but the ideas and beliefs they have about money. Every man should be taught how to handle ideas, rather than money, so that they serve him rather than have dominion over him.

The more Faith a man has in that which he is doing, toward which he is working, or that which he is presenting to others, the greater will be the manifestation of his own powers and capacity, the more efficient will be his performance of the work, and the greater will be his ability to influence others and to cause them to see things in the light of his own earnest belief and interest. Faith arouses and sustains Enthusiasm; lack of Faith deadens and inhibits it; UnFaith and positive Disbelief kill it. It is clear that the first step toward the cultivation and development of Enthusiasm is that of the creation of Faith in the subject or object toward which you wish to manifest and express Enthusiasm. If you have no Faith in the subject or object of your activities, then you will never be able to manifest Enthusiasm concerning that subject or object; and if you are unable to manifest at least a fair degree of such Enthusiasm, then you will never be able to express your full energies or to manifest your full powers in those activities. Finally, if you are unable to express your energies to the full and to manifest your powers adequately in those activities, then you will never be able to attain the full measure of success in your work connected with that particular subject or object. If you cannot arouse Faith and Enthusiasm in your work, you would do well to change your work so as to have it cover that in which you can arouse Faith and manifest Enthusiasm.

The soul in conscious touch with the Father-Mind and striving to fulfill the divine law brings the power of true words to bear in the purifying cleansing of its faculties. The necessity of abiding in the I AM in order to bear much fruit is affirmed. When our Faith attaches itself to outer things, instead of the spiritual I AM, it ceases to draw vitality from the one and only source of life, divine Principle. The only door to this life is the I AM. This abiding is a conscious centering of the mind in the depths within us by means of repeated affirmations of our Faith and trust in it. This day-by-day repeating of affirmations finally opens a channel of intelligent communication with the silent forces at the depths of Being; thoughts and words flow forth from there, and an entirely new source of power is developed in the man. When the thought or "word" of Truth from the supreme I AM of consciousness becomes an abiding fact in our mind, we need no longer strive in external ways. We have but to express a deep desire in the soul and it is fulfilled.

There is a life within that has no limit; it is the life more abundant . . the life that every awakened mind has sought with heart and soul; it is the life from which all great things proceed; the source of everything that has real value and high worth. Faith opens the door to this life and takes man into the sacred sanctuary within, to enter this life is to be filled with this life, and gain possession of all that this life may contain.

The man with his Subconscious filled with belief and Faith in his non-success, and in the inevitable failure of his efforts . . the man whose Confident Expectation is that of non-success, failure and inability, and whose Expectant Attention is directed toward such an outcome and the incidents and circumstances leading up to it, . . is like a man in the water who is swimming against the stream. He is opposing the strong current, and his every effort is counteracted and overcome by the adverse forces of the stream. Likewise, the man whose Subconscious is saturated with the conviction of ultimate victory and final success . . whose Confident Expectation is directed toward that end, and whose Expectant Attention is ever on the look-out for things tending to realize his inner beliefs . . is like the swimmer who is moving in the direction of the current. Such a man not only is not really opposed by the forces of the stream, but, instead, has these forces at work aiding him. The importance of having the Faith, Confident Expectation and Expectant Attention of the Subconscious directed toward your success, achievement and successful ultimate accomplishment . . and the importance of not having these mighty forces operative against yourself . . may be realized when you stop to consider that in the one case you have three-quarters of your mental equipment and power operating in your favor, and in the other case you have that three-quarters operating against you. And that three-quarters, in either case, not only is working actively during your waking hours, but also "works while you sleep." To lose the assistance of that three-quarters would be a serious matter, would it not? But far more serious is it to have that three-quarters actually working against you . . having it on the side of the enemy! This is just what happens when the Subconscious gets into action under the influence of wrongly directed Faith, Expectant Attention and Confident Expectation.

If Faith is moving in the wrong direction, moving with a negative Faith in evil, the only thing that needs to be done is to replace it with Faith in good. Dr. C. O. Southard says: "Faith is not subject to argument or experiment. A person either believes or disbelieves; and since that Faith is fixed in his Subconscious, it can only be altered by the person "Him"self, by his own efforts." Through the conscious Mind, we analyze the character of our Faith and make our decision. By using our will, we give attention to that which is good. What we give attention to becomes a moving force in our lives. Our Faith in good expands and grows with use.

The general conception of Faith . . the idea of Faith held by most persons . . is that it is an emotional state independent of, if not indeed actually contrary to Reason. This idea arises by reason of the tendency to view Faith only from one particular angle. If Faith were subjected to an "all around" view, the observer changing his position and shifting his viewpoint in his observation, it would be seen that while Faith often seems to transcend Reason and to be independent of its reports, yet it is not contrary to or opposed to Reason, and, in fact, depends largely upon Reason for its direction and application.

The mind of the child it is quite open to original impressions, and quite disposed to exercise Faith and belief concerning ideas presented to it, provided that these ideas do not conflict with those already accepted by it; but, also, like the mind of the child, it will hold fast to these ideas when they have been accepted as truth and forcibly impressed upon it, and will find it difficult to accept or act upon ideas opposed to them. Like the child mind, also, it readily forms habits of belief, thought, and action, and when these are once "set" it requires much work to change them or to reverse their action. We have evidences of this fact in our everyday lives . . you, yourself, can testify to its truth. Like nearly every other person, you have found yourself strongly influenced by silly, irrational, superstitious ideas, notions and habits of thought and action, long after you have thoroughly convinced yourself that such superstitions have no basis in fact or in truth. Your conscious mentality frees itself from the bonds of the superstition, but when you come to the test you find within yourself, deep down in your mental and emotional being, a distinct, definite and positive tendency to act according to the old belief or notion. You feel the pull of the Subconscious upon your Will, and it often requires the greatest exercise of Will-power to overcome that subconscious influence. The subconscious mentality must be "re-educated" before it will cease to protest and pull against your conscious reasoning mind.

You do not have to make anything. Mind makes it. You have only to speak the word. What is it that you want? You must know that. What will you have? You are the chooser. Definitely decide on what you want. Then as definitely declare that it is "done unto you now." Do not think of yourself as struggling to make something. Just think of yourself as the one who is starting the train of causation that is to bring you something. Put your word out with confidence, knowing that it is not you but Spirit that is to do the work. "Ye shall know the truth; and the TRUTH SHALL MAKE YOU FREE." The law of mind does all the work. Today declare, "I have Faith in the power of the law. I believe that all is mind, everywhere manifesting itself as the life and soul of things. I believe that all things and forms are responsive to my will because of the intelligence of the One Mind that dwells in them. I believe that my word goes forth to control my conditions. I believe that my word is the soul of the thing I desire and takes on its body when and where it is best. I believe that my word has power. I believe that my word registers in Creative Mind. I know now that this word that I AM speaking is being taken up by the All-Mind to be acted upon with all power and all intelligence. I have Faith in the power of my word to find its place in the Creative thought. I have Faith that it is there. The work is already done in my own consciousness. I feel satisfied. It is done." Then rest your case with the Creative Mind. " The truth shall make you free."

Live in the Faith that all things are working out right, and you will draw all things into the pathway of right; all things will go with you and do the right things for you. There is nothing strange about this, because the power of Faith is invincible. Faith is in touch with the world of unbounded power, therefore can do all things.

For him who would be rich, there is riches; and he who expects nothing shall equally be blessed by the law, for verily his Faith shall have its reward. "He sends his sun and his rain upon the just and the unjust, the evil and the good." Each of us makes his own sunrise and his own sunset. Each soars or crawls as his thought decrees.

A simple word of blessing poured out upon that which we have or that which we can conceive as possible for us as sons of the all-providing God (consciousness) will at least begin to release the superabundance of Spirit substance, and we shall have an inner confidence and Faith in the providence of our Father.

To keep your Faith in the world, look for good. You cannot look two ways at once; and "if your eye be single, your whole body will be full of light." The world grows better as we grow better. We see only those things that most interest us. We must therefore seek higher and finer interests if we are to have Faith in the world. Never forget that the world becomes to you just what you become to it. The law of mind is that we get out of the Universal just what we put into it. If, therefore, you would have Faith in the world, turn your mind to the good there is in it. Soon you will begin to attract around you those who are most like you in mental attitudes. They, too, will see the good; and, as you will be mutually associated, you will soon find that you have Faith in the world because you not only saw the good and thought the good but you have now actually demonstrated the good.

A study of the world of men will disclose the fact that those men who eventually succeed, who "arrive" ultimately, who "do things," are marked by this deep intuitive Faith in themselves, and by their Confident Expectation of ultimate success. These men rise superior to the incidents of temporary defeat; they use these failures as stepping-stones to ultimate victory. They are living expressions of Henley's "Invictus" . . they, indeed, are the Masters of their Fate, the Captains of their Souls! Such men are never really defeated; like rubber balls, they have that "bounce" which causes them to rise triumphantly after each fall . . the harder they are "thrown down," the higher do they rise on the rebound. Such men are always possible . . nay, probable and certain . . victors, so long as they maintain this intuitive Faith in Self, or Self Confidence; it is only when this is lost that they are really defeated or destroyed.

Faith is interior understanding; Faith can look beyond the world of sense and see things as they are; Faith can see what is in the real, what can be done through the realization of the real, what ought to be done to express the real, and how this may be done now; or what should be done now to work up to the high ideals we may have in view.

When Faith is directed toward anything or anybody, it acts of its own volition. Faith draws to us that toward which our Faith is directed.

Learn to live life day by day. Never live tomorrow except by happy anticipation. To dread tomorrow is to demonstrate a tomorrow to be dreaded. If today is not all you wish it to be, rise above it in thought and declare your Faith in all the good to come. Then it must come.

The foundation of every work is an idea. Faith is that quality of mind which makes the idea stand out as real, not only to ourself but to others. When others have Faith in the thing you are doing, making, or selling, they see it as real and worthwhile. Then your success and your prosperity are assured. Whatever you put into substance along with Faith will work out in manifestation in your world. You demonstrate prosperity by an understanding of the prosperity law and by having Faith in it. Faithfulness and earnestness in the application of the prosperity law will assure you of success. If you have Faith in outer things, you are building shadows without substance, shadows that cease as soon as your supporting thought is withdrawn from them, forms that will pass away and leave you nothing. Do not have Faith in anything less than God (consciousness), in anything other than the one Mind, for when your Faith is centered there, you are building for eternity. Mind and the ideas of Mind will never pass away. There will never be an end to God (consciousness). There will never be an end to Truth, which God (consciousness) is. There will never be an end to substance, which God (consciousness) is. Build with the divine substance. Cultivate Faith in realities. We must find a way to connect ideas of substance with ideas of material expression. This is accomplished by Faith through prayer according to our decree. We are always decreeing, sometimes consciously, often unconsciously. With every thought and word we are increasing or diminishing the activity of substance. The resulting manifestation conforms to our thought.

Jesus knew that the Law of Faith works negatively as well as positively. When a man says, "There are no opportunities for one my age. Nobody wants a man over fifty. The cards are stacked against me. I never get the breaks. I am not well enough to take a job," and he believes, that . . . which he saith (accepts it as true), shall come to pass. What he believes will continue to manifest in his affairs. God (consciousness) is not unkind or unfriendly, but He works through Law. Life responds to us by corresponding to our states of thought. It gives to us according to our expectations. The Law is impersonal. It works the way we use It.

The law cannot fail to operate when once set in operation in the right way. All men who have prospered used the law, for there is no other way. Perhaps they were not conscious of following definite spiritual methods, yet they have in some way set the law in operation and reaped the benefit of its unfailing action. Others have to struggle to accomplish the same things. You will not have to wait for seedtime and harvest when you learn to use the power of your mind. When you have the consciousness in which your ideas are tangible, all your demands will be quickly fulfilled by the higher law. Throw into your ideas all the life and power of your concentrated thought, and they will be clothed with reality. Your conscious cooperation is necessary to the fullest results in the working of the universal law of increase. Use your talent, whatever it may be, in order to increase it. Have Faith in the law. Do not reason too much but forge ahead in Faith and boldness. If you let yourself think of any person or any outer condition as hindering your increase, this becomes a hindrance to you. Keep your eyes on the abundant inner reality. Do not let the outer appearance cause you to falter.

What do you want! What do you expect These are the decisive factors in the living of your life. Behind you lie the broken things of yesterday. Forget them. Before you is dawn and the day. What shall come forth out of the unrolled parchment of the future? It is for you to decide. You hold tomorrow in the hollow of your hand. God (consciousness) is on your side. Life is on your side. Eternity is on your side; Life never ends. All things are possible to him that believes. "Only have Faith; and thy Faith shall save thee." Believe, believe! EXPECT, EXPECT!!

Faith, in its essence and fundamental substance, may be said to be beyond Reason . . to transcend Reason. Yet, without the employment of Reason and experience, Faith degenerates into mere blind credulity. While not dependent upon Reason for its basic foundation, and while not having Reason as its fount and spring, yet Faith needs employ Reason as its useful instrument of manifestation and expression, and must use the sign-posts of Reason as guides pointing out the road over which it travels. It is equally true that Reason must be based upon Faith, for, of itself it has no ultimate foundation. Reason and Faith are not antagonistic, when they are rightly understood: rather are they brothers-in-arms, each helpful and useful to the other. The ideal is the well-balanced coordination and correlation of Reason and Faith.

Faith is an attitude of the whole Mind but fulfillment depends upon how deeply it is embedded in the Subconscious. Out of the heart (Subconscious Mind) are the issues of life, said Jesus. No matter how much we may know intellectually, or how fervently we may pray, we always attract those things which we really are. The Law of Faith works both ways. If it is centered in the desirable, we attract the desirable. If it is centered in the undesirable, we attract the undesirable. That is the Law of Polarity.

When you first begin to think of God (consciousness) as everywhere-present substance, your mind will not always adhere continuously to the idea. You need to develop certain stabilizing ideas. One of them is continuity or loyalty to Truth. Love sticks to the thing on which it has set its mind. Nothing so tends to stabilize and unify all as love. And nothing is so important as sticking to the ideal and never giving up the work we have set out to accomplish. Perhaps some adverse condition of your own thought has prevented a full demonstration. Do not let this swerve you from your loyalty to the law. You may seem to attain results very slowly. That is the best reason for sticking closely to your ideal and not changing your mind. Be loyal to Principle. The adverse condition will break up. The true light will come and the invisible substance you have been Faithfully affirming will begin to reveal itself to you in all its fullness of good. It will destroy your fears, stop your worries, and change your finances.

Your getting well depends upon your beginning to think . . and act . . in a Certain Way. The way a person thinks about things is determined by what he believes about them. His thoughts are determined by his Faith, and the results depend upon his making a personal application of his Faith. If a person has Faith in the efficacy of a medicine, and is able to apply that Faith to himself, that medicine will certainly cause him to be cured. But though his Faith be great, he will not be cured unless he applies it to himself. Many sick people have Faith for others but none for themselves. So, if he has Faith in a system of diet, and can personally apply that Faith, it will cure him. And if he has Faith in prayers and affirmations and personally applies his Faith, prayers and affirmations will cure him. Faith, personally applied, cures. And no matter how great the Faith or how persistent the thought, it will not cure without personal application. The Science of Being Well, then, includes the two fields of thought and action. To be well it is not enough that a person should merely think in a Certain Way. He must apply his thought to himself, and he must express and externalize it in his outward life by acting in the same way that he thinks.

Someone has defined Faith as "the unconditional acceptance of the truth of our affirmations and an absolute belief that our desires will be fulfilled. "Faith is not presumption but assumption. It is believing something which the conscious Mind says is not true.

In the exoteric teachings and doctrine, Faith is advocated and demanded because of its claimed power to place man in close relationship with the Supreme Being, and to render possible a spiritual rapport or sympathetic accord with Divine Power. It is there held that the Supreme Being demands Faith as a prerequisite of the bestowal of favors and gifts. In the esoteric teaching and doctrine, however, while Faith is still more earnestly insisted upon as a prerequisite of Attainment, there is not this rather naive and primitive explanation: instead, Faith is explained as that act by means of which the individual soul enters into a fuller recognition and realization of its essential identity with, and contact with the Divine Principle, and thus is enabled to unfold and to manifest those divine powers which are inherent and latent within its nature. Faith, in the exoteric sense, is a "rapport," i. e., "sympathetic accord" relationship: in the esoteric, it is rather a "rapprochement," or "act of re-approach or coming-together again after a separation," or "act or fact of again coming or being drawn near or together." Even those not accepting the doctrine of the essential identity of the individual soul with the Universal Soul, and who occupy the agnostic position regarding this question, must be forced to admit as logically sound the argument that if the individual soul is potentially divine, then the act of earnest, positive Faith in its potentially divine nature and possibilities must serve to unfold into manifestation such powers. The esoteric doctrine, however, does not rest merely upon this undoubtedly logically sound premise or proposition . . it bases its chief claim upon the fact that the soul which proceeds "as if this were so" soon begins to manifest its powers to such an extent that further doubt is impossible. Thus the proof or the esoteric teaching and doctrine is, at the last, a matter of actual personal experience. Cries the mystic: "Taste, only taste; taste, and you will know the virtue of the Wine!"

The subject of Faith should be applied especially to the demonstrations of prosperity. It is our starting point in building a prosperity consciousness and making our world as we would have it. We all have Faith, for it is innate in every man. Our question is how we may put it to work in our affairs. In a sense Faith represents substance. With it, it is possible to possess a reality that cannot be seen, touched, or comprehended by any of the outer senses. It is Faith when we are fully conscious of "things not seen" and have the "assurance of things" not yet manifest. In other words, Faith is that consciousness in us of the reality of the invisible substance and of the attributes of mind by which we lay hold of it. We must realize that the mind makes things real. "Just a thought" or "just a mere idea," we sometimes lightly say, little thinking that these thoughts and ideas are the eternal realities from which we build our life and our world.

I can speak the word of Peace, Health, or Prosperity, but unless my feeling supports the word that I speak, it accomplishes nothing. It is only when my word and my feeling unite that I become One with the Power. Why is this true? Because feeling is the shock that sets the Divine Energy in motion. There is a powerful Spiritual Law at work

Your Faith Is Your Fortune: Your Unlimited Power

here. It doesn't make any difference what your problem or difficulty may be, if you will bring your Faith and your feeling to bear upon it, if you will realize that right now and always, there is an Infinite "Power waiting to fulfill your slightest or greatest wish, you don't need to seek the solution. It will seek you.

Your desire to be your best has expanded your Faith into the Faith of the Universe which knows no failure, and has brought you into conscious realization that you are not a victim of the universe, but a part of it. Consequently you are able to recognize that there is that within yourself which is able to make conscious contact with the Universal Law, and enables you to press all the particular laws of Nature, whether visible or invisible, into serving your particular demand or desire. Thereby you find yourself Master, not a slave, of any situation. Troward tells us that this Mastering is to be "accomplished by knowledge, and the only knowledge which will afford this purpose in all its measureless immensity is the knowledge of the personal element in universal spirit," and its reciprocity to our own personality. In other words, the words you think, the personality you feel yourself to be, are all reproductions in miniature of God (consciousness), "or specialized universal spirit." All your word-thoughts were God (consciousness) word-forms before they were yours. The words you use are the instruments . . channels . . through which the creative energy takes form. Naturally, this sensitive Creative Power can only reproduce in accordance with the instrument through which it passes. All disappointments and failures are the result of endeavoring to think one thing and produce another.

There is nothing you cannot be if you have Faith enough to accept the fact that what you are seeking is already yours. The fact that you can visualize a changed condition is proof of the Spiritual Reality of it.

Faith is the underlying principle of that remarkable quality of the human mind which is known as Enthusiasm. It is its essence, it is its substance, it is its actuating principle. Without Faith there can be no manifestation of Enthusiasm. Without Faith there can be no expression of the activities of Enthusiasm. Without Faith there can be no exhibition of the energies of Enthusiasm. Without Faith the quality of Enthusiasm remains dormant, latent and static . . Faith is needed to arouse it, to render it active, to cause it to become dynamic. Moreover, the Faith required for the manifestation and expression of Enthusiasm must be positive Faith . . Faith in the successful outcome of the undertaking . . Faith exhibiting its positive phases . . Faith in the attainment of that which is desirable and which is regarded as good. You can never manifest Enthusiasm toward that which you confidently expect to be a failure, nor toward that which you feel will bring undesirable results and effects. Negative Faith has no power to arouse Enthusiasm: the presence of Positive Faith is necessary to awaken this wonderful latent mental or spiritual force.

Fear is man's worse enemy for you attract what you fear. It is Faith turned upside down. It is really Faith in evil instead of good. "Why are ye fearful! Oh! Ye of little Faith?" The fearless, unfettered mind attracts to itself all good. Whatever you desire or require is already on your pathway. "Before ye call I have answered."

But you ask, "How can I speak the word of Faith when I have little or no Faith?" Every living thing has Faith in something or somebody. Faith is that quality of Power which gives the Creative Energy a corresponding vitality, and the vitality in the word of Faith you use causes it to take corresponding physical form. Even intense fear is alive with Faith. You fear poverty and loneliness because you believe them possible for you. It is the Faith which understands that every creation had its birth in the womb of thought-words, that gives you dominion over all things, your lesser self included, and this feeling of Faith is increased and intensified through observing what it does. Your constant observation should be of your state of consciousness when you did; not when you hoped you might, but feared it was too good to be true. How did you feel that time when you simply had to bring yourself into a better frame of mind and did, or you had to have a certain thing and got it? Live these experiences over again and again . . mentally . . until you really feel in touch with the self which knows and does, and then the best there is, is yours.

Faith is the starting point of every affirmation, prayer, and treatment; but without recognition of it as evidence of the Father Within without awareness of the closeness of our relationship to "Him", without acceptance of His promises, without the realization of the Omnipresence of God (consciousness), it is likely to end as wishful thinking, daydreaming, or mere desire.

I know of a woman who had been a coward all her life, particularly about finances. She worried all the time about money. She came into this Truth, realized how she had limited herself, and suddenly made the giant swing into Faith. She commenced to trust God (consciousness) and not the external for her supply. She followed her intuitive leads about spending. If any of her clothes made her feel poor, she would discard them at once, getting something new to make her feel rich. She had very little money, but gave one-tenth to good works. She was winding herself up into a new vibration. Very soon, things commenced to change on the external. A woman, on whom she had no claim, who was merely an old friend of her family, left her a thousand dollars. A few months later, another thousand came in. Then a big door opened for her supply and many thousands came in. She had tapped her invisible supply from the Bank of the Universe. She had looked to God (consciousness) only for her supply, then the channels opened. The point I am bringing out is, that she had lost all anxiety about money matters. She had established in her subconscious, the firm conviction, that her supply come from God (consciousness), and it never failed. Man is an instrument for Infinite Intelligence to work through. It will express though him as success, happiness, abundance, health and perfect self-expression, unless fear and anxiety make a short circuit.

Turn the power of praise upon whatever you wish to increase. Give thanks that it is now fulfilling your ideal. The Faithful law, Faithfully observed, will reward you. You can praise yourself from weakness to strength, from ignorance to intelligence, from lack to affluence, from sickness to health.

If your prosperity does not become manifest as soon as you pray and affirm God (consciousness) as your substance, your supply, and your support, refuse to give up. A continuity of effort is necessary. Show your Faith by keeping up the work. You do not have to work laboriously in the outer to accomplish. Most of us rush around trying to work out our problems for ourself and in our way, with one thought, one vision: the material thing we seek. You need to devote more time to silent meditation. Remember that substance ideas with which you are working are eternal. The same ideas that formed this planet in the first place sustain it now.

The wise teachers of the race have for centuries taught that this Faith in the Real Self, in the "I AM I," will enable the individual to convert into the instruments of his success even those circumstances which apparently are destined to defeat his purposes; and to transmute into beneficent agencies even those inimical forces which beset him on all sides. They have discovered, and passed on to their followers, the knowledge, that such a Faith is a spiritual power, a living force, which when trusted and rightly employed will annihilate the opposition of outward circumstances, or else convert them into workers for good.

The average person is resenter, a resister, or a regretter. They resent people they know and people they don't know. They resist everything from daylight saving up. They regret what they did or what they didn't do. It is very wearing to be with people. They exhaust all their friends. It is because they are not living in the wonderful NOW and are losing all the tricks in the game of life. It is heaven to be unafraid and to live fully in the NOW; that is, to be fearless in using what we have, knowing back to us is the abundance of the spheres to draw upon. We know that fearless Faith and the spoken word release this supply. The power of the word was known in Egypt thousands of years ago.

Jesus knew that the Law of Faith works negatively as well as positively. When a man says, "There are no opportunities for one my age. Nobody wants a man over fifty. The cards are stacked against me. I never get the breaks. I am not well enough to take a job," and he believes, that ... which he saith (accepts it as true), shall come to pass. What he believes will continue to manifest in his affairs. God (consciousness) is not unkind or unfriendly, but He works through Law. Life responds to us by corresponding to our states of thought. It gives to us according to our expectations. The Law is impersonal. It works the way we use It.

When you sow seed thoughts for some special purpose, hold it in mind until you have acquired your desire in objective form. You cannot fail if you want anything hard enough to make the proper mental effort to impress your desire on your subconscious mind. It has been commonly supposed that the dreamer is a failure, but he who builds his future in his imagination with Faith and purpose, never fails to realize his desire. Of course, merely wishing for anything or just to let your fancy run riot is wasted effort, because when you wish you do not believe you can obtain your wishes and you are really saying to your inner power, "I certainly would like to have so and so, but it is beyond my means." To use your mental powers in this way is to sow failure. Be positive, do not say, "I'd like to have," but, "It is MINE." Whenever you claim anything by Faith never go behind that statement. Let every effort of yours be mentally listed as carrying you nearer your goal. When Jesus said, "As thy Faith is, so be it unto you," He made a statement that is today considered a SCIENTIFIC FACT.

Many have learned how to hold the truth about health steadily in Faith even in the midst of the most adverse appearances. They clearly understand that they are not telling falsehoods when they deny sickness right in the face of the appearance of it. Persons who are quickened spiritually can do very much greater works through the law of Faith than those who are still in the material consciousness. Once having discerned the power of Spirit, we should be on our guard and send forth on every occasion exalted ideas of the spiritual.

The entire Book of Hebrews is devoted to Faith: "Faith is enduring as seeing him who is invisible." And "Faith is the substance of things hoped for." "Unto us was this good news preached, as well as unto them, but it did not profit them because it was not mixed with Faith." Good news is desire fulfilled. If desire is not mixed with Faith, it is of no avail, for Faith is the awareness of the reality of the desire's fulfillment. You see, creation is finished, and we only become aware of increasing portions of it. The absence of Faith would be to deny the reality of the state assumed. If you limit yourself to your physical senses which contradict everything you desire, then Faith will be unknown to you. But Faith will make real that which is invisible.

The most important part of demonstrating is showing fearless Faith. "I will go before thee and make the crooked places straight! I will break in pieces the gates of brass and cut in sunder the bars of iron." The Bible is talking about states of consciousness. "The gates of brass" and "bars of iron," are your doubts, fears, resentments and anxieties. The gates of brass and bars of iron are of our own making and come from our own vain imaginings, a belief in evil. There is a story of a herd of wild elephants: they were corralled in an enclosure but the men had no way of keeping them in, so they dug stakes and put a rope all around the enclosure. The elephants thought they could not get out. They could have just walked over the rope and stepped out but they had the illusion that the rope kept them in. This is the way with people: doubt and fear is a rope stretched around their consciousness. It makes it impossible for them to walk out into clear thinking.

The law of the subconscious mind is suggestion. The subconscious mind does not think, reason, balance, judge or reject. It simply accepts all suggestions furnished by the conscious mind; whether they be good or evil, constructive or destructive. Therefore the secret of success is to store your subconscious mind with desire, ambition, courage, determination, enthusiasm and Faith in yourself. Add to these indispensable attributes love for your fellow man and Faith in the ultimate good of all things. Have Faith in your inherent power to achieve; it is Faith in yourself that attracts success. If you do not limit your capacities they will have no limit. The Universal Mind sees all, knows all and can do all. We share in this absolute power exactly to the extent of our Faith, belief and purpose. Our mental attitude is the magnet that draws to us everything we need to bring our desires into being.

The man who wants the inner life to spring forth must believe in the reality of the omnipresent spiritual life and must exercise his Faith by invoking in prayer the presence of the invisible but omnipresent God (consciousness). This reveals to consciousness the glory of Spirit, and the soul has witness of itself of a power that it knew not. In Spirit all things are fulfilled now. The moment a concept enters the mind, the thing conceived is consummated through the law that governs the action of ideas. The spiritual-minded take advantage of this law and affirm the completeness of this ideal, regardless of outer appearances. This stimulates the energy in the thought process and gives it power beyond estimate.

Faith does not stand apart from the physical world, waiting to minister to certain obscure spiritual wants only; Faith is ready to turn its power into everything and has the power to produce success through everything; but Faith will not cooperate with those things that are looked down upon and condemned by man.

Faith without works (or action) is dead." Active Faith impresses the subconscious with expectance and you keep your contact with the Universal Intelligence. Just as Wall Street watches the market, we must watch our Faith market. Often the Faith market is down. Sometimes it goes down and down until a crash comes: some unhappy situation which we could have prevented. We realized we followed reason instead of intuition.

Faith may be defined to be the power of perceiving spiritual realities that lie above and beyond the range of the senses, and a confidence in those higher truths. This is essentially the definition of it given by the unknown Kabalistic author of the Epistle to the Hebrews. Faith is the source of all spiritual power. The end and purpose of all education is, and will be of our present studies, the achievement of spiritual development and the attainment of a truly spiritual mode and habit of thought. In other words, our aim should be expressed in the comprehensive prayer, "Lord, increase our Faith"

There is no better time to start the growth of the Faith consciousness than when you are quietly resting or just before you fall to sleep. State firmly that you do have Faith, that your Faith is growing, that you will awaken with renewed hope and peace, and the sleepless self will carry your thought to the ultimate conclusion. You will then awake to new courage and a more positive attitude of expectancy. As soon as you awake, think how beautiful everything is, how well you are and will continue to be. In the morning you can give yourself perhaps the best treatment because you usually feel so refreshed that you do not have anything in consciousness to contradict your word.

"**And all things, whatsoever ye shall ask in prayer,** believing, ye shall receive". "Therefore I say unto you, what things soever ye desire, when ye pray, believe that ye receive them, and ye shall have them". In this parable he shows that only those who have prepared for their good (thereby showing active Faith) will bring the manifestation to pass.

Faith is the substance of things hoped for; Faith enters into the very life and substance of that which is desired, thereby finding the substance and gaining possession of the coveted treasure.

In the "mustard seed" stage, my Faith is like a little candle in the Mind. It gives forth a certain amount of light. But it is governed by impersonal law; it works the way I use it. If it works slowly for me at first, that is because my expectations and mental equivalents are small. I need to step them up. I know that a little steam will lift the lid of a tea kettle but a lot of steam will lift tons. The Law of Faith is just that simple: With what measure ye mete, it shall be measured to you again. The manifestation of my Faith is not measured by the size of my Faith but by the acceptance, belief, or mental equivalent which I hold.

The man who has Faith in himself not only brings under his control and direction those wonderful powers of his subconscious mentality, and the full power of his conscious mental faculties and instruments, but also tends to inspire a similar feeling in the minds and hearts of those other individuals with whom he comes in contact in the course of his pursuit of the objects of his endeavors. An intuitive perception and realization of one's own powers and energies, capacity and efficiency, possibilities and capabilities, is an essential attribute of the individual who is destined to success.

Many people have found that the statement "I owe no man anything but love" has helped them greatly to counteract this thought of debt. As they used the words their minds were opened to an inflow of divine love and they Faithfully cooperated with the divine law of forgiveness in thought, word, and deed. They built up such a strong consciousness of the healing and enriching power of God's (consciousness's) love that they could live and work peacefully and profitably with their associates. Thus renewed constantly in health, in Faith, and in integrity, they were able to meet every obligation that came to them. The statement "I owe no man anything but love" does not mean that we can disclaim owing our creditors money or try to evade the payment of obligations we have incurred. The thing denied is the burdensome thought of debt or of lack. The work of paying debts is an inner work having nothing to do with the debts already owed but with the wrong thoughts that produced them. When one holds to the right ideas, burdensome debts will not be contracted.

If we want examples of fearless Faith, go to the circus! The circus people perform seemingly impossible feats because they think they can, and see themselves doing it. Faith means that you can see yourself receiving all these things that you desire. "I will give to thee the land that thou seest." You can never do a thing you cannot see yourself doing, or fill a place you cannot see yourself filling – not visualizing, making mental picture (this is a mental process and often brings wrong and limited results); it must be a spiritual realization, a feeling that you are already there; be in its vibration.

Hold ever in mind an image of the ideal you are seeking to make manifest. That image will become a central living magnet which will begin to draw to you the experiences that must be encountered and the conditions that must be overcome before the ideal can be attained. Concentrate all the forces of your being on the undoubted duty of the moment; then the numberless wants will be forgotten, and the troubles and uncertainties of life will pass away. The pathway of today is illumined by the experience you have gained from the yesterdays; and the light that dispels the mystery surrounding the present gives greater knowledge, which will shine with increased brightness tomorrow. The things that are true, the things that are good, and all that is helpful, will gravitate to you only in proportion to the degree that you desire and invite them. Though the unwelcome duties of the hour may cause unrest, and the barren outlook of the future discourage, have Faith in your power to triumph over all things which would wrest from your grasp the glorious heritage. Have Faith in the harmony, the love and the goodness of the immutable laws which govern life and destiny and change.

"Where There Is A Will There Is A Way." The reason this is so is that the Will can make a way if given the chance to secure the assistance of aiding forces. The more it is developed the higher the way to which it will lead. When everything looks gloomy and discouraging, then is the time to show what you are made of by rejoicing that you can control your moods by making them as calm, serene and bright as if prosperity were yours. "Be Faithful in sowing the thought seeds of success, in perfect trust that the sun will not cease to shine and bring a generous harvest in one season."

Edison was the man who had Faith in the laws of electricity. He knew what could be with it if it were harnessed and directed. It seemed to have intelligence of its own. He created dynamo through which it would work, after years of patience and loving absorption in his work. Now this power lights the world, for it is harnessed and directed. Jesus Christ taught man to harness and direct thought. He knew that fear was as dangerous as uncontrolled electrical forces. Words and thoughts must be handled with wisdom and understanding. The imagination is man's workshop, and an imagination running wild and building up fear pictures, is just about as safe as riding a bucking bronco.

Often we miss the fruit of Faith because we have not continued in Faith, or awaited the fulfillment of Faith. No farmer would plant his grain and not await his harvest. Instead he would make preparation for his harvest. He would plant his seed believing that he would receive. Even so a mother who has conceived a child trusts that interior growth which takes place and which is hid from her view, and prepares for the birth of the child, believing she has received. So, when we speak the word of Truth which is the seed of the ideal we wish to see manifest, we must believe we have, and with no doubt in the mind, trust that first growth which always takes place within, hid from view. Fear, doubt and uncertainty prevent the perfect "holding in mind" of the thing desired, and until it is established, or made firm, in mind it cannot take form in the external.

Cultivate true desire and perfect self control. The highest desire awakens in the heart the purest love . . the love which recognizes the vital relationship existing between nature and every human being. With the awakening of this love, unsuspected powers will be developed. You will gather to yourself new vigor, magnetism and force. Learn to control every impulse, passion and desire which spring up in the changeful heart. Maintain the attitude of the master. Be sincere, noble and upright, and have Faith in your power to overcome all obstacles which are to be met in the upward march to success. Let your zeal be broad and deep. When the opportunity comes for action, let your efforts be well directed, and with a force that conquers. Recognizing the beauty of the higher life, resolve to make each day's record better than that of the preceding one, to make each hour's effort a stepping stone by which you will rise to better things. Let your thoughts and desires ever roar upward. Let no mistrust of your powers cause you to hesitate, for the worthy exercise of the gifts you already recognize will bring you to a knowledge of others still more to be prized. The fulfillment of your highest aspirations is possible if you will control and make the best use of the forces within. Have no fear of placing before yourself impossible ideals. But in thinking of the goal you are to reach in the future, do not lose sight of the present. The one who looks to the future, unmindful of the present, may lose the opportunities of today and the possibilities of tomorrow. No promise of good to be done or of triumph to be achieved in the future can compensate for the neglect of the present.

Faith is the glass under the faucet; it is the water wheel under the fall; it is the windmill adjusted to the wind; it is the sunflower facing the sun; it is the ear at the telephone.

Faith proves the existence of God (consciousness) by elaborate appeals to the reason. Such appeals will be made as long as all human beings do not possess the precise union of imperfect knowledge and spiritual emotion necessary to give birth to uniformity of Faith. The question of the being of God (consciousness) is not a mere internal sentiment; it is a philosophical doctrine, to be justified or rejected on grounds of reason. The very nature of Faith implies trust in an object. But whether that object be a real or an imaginary one is for reason to determine, if it can.

The life of man is large or small in proportion to his Faith, because it is through Faith that he touches the source of life and receives life. Likewise, all the attainments and achievements of man are large or small in proportion to his Faith. "According to your Faith," that is the law that determines everything.

"Ask, believing, thou shalt receive!" We know that our beliefs or expectancies are impressed upon the subconscious and carried out. We might say, if you ask, not believing, you will not receive. Faith creates expectancy. This Infinite Intelligence upon which man draws his supply is called, by Jesus Christ, "your Heavenly Father." The Father within, He described as a kind, loving parent desirous of pouring all good things upon His children. "Fear not, little flock, 'tis your Father's good pleasure to give you the kingdom." He taught that God's (consciousness's) law was simply a law of love and good-will. "Love your neighbor as yourself" – "Do unto others as you would be done by." Any violation of the law of love causes a shot circuit. "The way of the transgressor is hard." God (consciousness) is immutable law – "I AM the Lord (law), I change not."

George W. Wilson says:

"**Possession follows the feeling** that you do possess the things desired, and that feeling is made stronger if you will express gratitude for the possession." "What things soever ye desire . . . believe that ye receive them, and ye shall have them." When one is grateful for something he has not yet seen or touched or experienced as the result of his conviction that it already exists, his gratitude will hasten its arrival. Have you ever noticed that praise of a dog brings out the best in him and that praise of a man inspires him to be and to do his best? So it is with Faith.

The "godless" are they who are goodless, even though they may be members of churches and make a great profession of Faith in God.

The "godly" are they who are goodly even though they make no profession of religion.

The complainers and bewailers are the Faithless and unbelieving. Those who deny or belittle the power of good, and in their lives and actions affirm and magnify the power of evil, are the only real atheists.

We did not know that words and thoughts are a form of dynamite, and should be handled carefully, with wisdom and understanding. We hurled out into the ethers, words of anger, resentment or self-pity, then wondered why life was so hard. Why not experiment with Faith; trust this invisible God-power (consciousness) and "In nothing be anxious," but "in everything by prayer and thanksgiving, let your requests be made known unto God (consciousness)." Could anything be more simple and direct? Anxiety forms you have become habits. The old thought forms you have built up in the subconscious, hang on like barnacles on an ocean liner. But the ocean liner is put in dry-dock once in a while to have the barnacles scraped off, so, your mental barnacles will have to go though the same process. The dry-dock is a big situation.

Health, wealth and love depend upon our Faith in the Spirit and our allegiance to the law. Therefore, if you feel separated from good; if you are inclined to condemn yourself for past acts, saying, "This is just what I ought to expect," and accepting it as inevitable; if you submit meekly to suffering; if you think that your word lacks power because you have done what is wrong; if in any way you have a sense of separation from Spirit, then forgive yourself.

Doubt not. Doubt is one of the malignant forces that attempt to operate against Faith. If ye have Faith and doubt not . . . whatsoever things ye shall ask in prayer, believing, ye shall receive. . . . Whosoever . . . shall not doubt in his heart, but shall believe that those things which he saith shall come to pass; he shall have whatsoever he saith. We open the Mind through Faith and close it through doubt. A kingdom divided against itself shall fall.

With spiritual law there is only the now. Before you call you are answered, for "time and space are but a dream," and your blessing is there waiting for you to release it by Faith and the word. "Choose you this day whom ye will serve," fear or Faith. In every act prompted by fear lies the germ of its own defeat.

If you have sufficient Faith in your own ability and in the universal force with which you cooperate, if you feel that the best things the world can give are none too good for you, that you have the knowledge, the talent and the executive ability to move things, to influence people and command attention, if you live in this permanent state of mind, you will draw to you the material counterpart of every thought demand. Put your mind in harmony with the Infinite Source and in line of correspondence with the things you seek, then you will receive impressions in regard to the steps to be taken to reach the goal desired. The less you depend upon others and the more you trust your enlightened reason, the clearer you will see and the more strength you will have to stand alone. You will realize that as an inseparable part of the infinite power of good, you may command the qualities needed to accomplish wonderful results. You will receive an impulse and inspiration that will be finer and more effective. You will advance to higher planes of usefulness and grow in knowledge and understanding. Keep yourself positive, and banish all unwelcome thoughts that seek entrance. Study yourself, your relation to environment, your desires and possibilities. Surround yourself by those who have kindred desires and talents. Strengthen your forces by keeping in touch with those who can help you to realize your ideals. There is no one thing in life, within the range of possibility, which you cannot accomplish, if you will recognize the power and efficiency of well directed thought, supported by an unwavering Faith, resolution and persistent desire.

I know from experience that it is just a matter of choosing what we will have. This putting one's self into the actual position desired, is acceptance, or active Faith. We may affirm till doomsday and get no results, unless we at the same time, either consciously or subconsciously, see ourselves in possession. "Believe that ye have received "bears strongly upon this argument.

The more enthusiasm and Faith you are able to put into your picture, the more quickly it will come into visible form, and your enthusiasm is increased by keeping your desire secret. The moment you speak it to any living soul, that moment your power is weakened. Your power, your magnet of attraction is not that strong, and consequently cannot reach so far. The more perfectly a secret between your mind and your outer self is guarded, the more vitality you give your power of attraction. One tells one's troubles to weaken them, to get them off one's mind, and when a thought is given out, its power is dissipated. Talk it over with yourself, and even write it down, then destroy the paper. However, this does not mean that you should strenuously endeavor to compel the Power to work out your picture on the special lines that you think it should.

This method of repeating the word makes the word in all of its limitless meaning yours, because words are the embodiment of thoughts, and thought is creative; neither good nor bad, simply creative. This is the reason why Faith builds up and Fear destroys. "Only believe, and all things are possible unto you." It is Faith that gives you dominion over every adverse circumstance or condition. It is your word of Faith that sets you free; not Faith in any specific thing or act, but simple Faith in your best self in all ways. It is this ever-present Creative Power within the heart of the word that makes your health, your peace of mind, and your financial condition a reproduction of your most habitual thought. Try to believe and understand this, and you will find yourself Master of every adverse circumstance or condition, for you will become a Prince of Power.

Get busy with your Subconscious. Train it, educate it, re-educate it, direct it, incline it, teach it, suggest to it, along the lines of the Faith in Success and Power, and not those of the Faith in Failure and Weakness. Set it to work swimming with that current. The Subconscious is much given to Faith . . it lives on Faith, it acts upon Faith. Then see that you supply it with the right kind of Faith, and avoid as a pestilence that Faith which is based on Fear and is grounded in Failure and Despair. Think carefully . . and act!

The law of Faith is universal; it is just as powerful and just as available now as it ever has been, and every desire of our hearts is included in its rich promises to all men. God (consciousness) never gave poverty to one man and riches to another, neither has He ever brought sickness to you and health to your neighbor; Life, health and abundance are omnipresent. The only law of nature is the LAW OF SUPPLY. Poverty is unnatural; it is distinctly a man-made condition, brought about by the limits man places upon himself. God's (consciousness's) gifts are equally available to everyone. Health, Happiness, and Prosperity are not limited either to time, place or individual; they are a matter of consciousness and are attracted to those who understand and believe in their own inherent powers to achieve.

Faith is essentially Spiritual. Faith begins in the Mind but comes to fruition in the heart. Faith is not measured by our intellectual ability to call a thing done, but by the realization in the heart that it is done. Belief is of the intellect while Faith is of the heart. Many people believe that they are one and the same thing, but that is not true. Almost anyone can believe, but not everyone can exercise Faith. Without the power of Faith, belief is weak.

If you have an unfaltering purpose, and are determined to push your plans to completion, if you are not vexed or discouraged by those who oppose you, if you can always persist in your work and keep up enthusiasm, energy and Faith, you will draw to you an ever increasing power from the unseen, which will act on you and on other minds, establishing magnetic currents of sympathy which will awaken great confidence and hope and give the ability to achieve success. The greater the number who cooperate with you and give you their sympathy, the more power will you receive. The force you will obtain may be transmuted by thought, desire and will into a vital attractive power which, if wisely expended, will give unlimited capacity for material accomplishment. We are continually sending out a mental force which establishes invisible connections with other minds on the same plane of unfoldment; and to send out with this force an attractive influence will draw to us sympathetic thoughts which will aid us.

Faith, the conviction of a higher providing Source, is based upon spiritual logic or innate reason and on the certainty that an all-wise and all-powerful Creator's plan includes necessary provision for His offspring. When man emerges from the limitations of human consciousness and feels within him the stirring of Spirit, he finds that it is supremely logical and true that Spirit has provided for his supply and support.

When we exercise Faith, all doubt, all fear and all anxiety are absent; should these undesirable mental states appear, we may know that our minds are thinking about the surface of things instead of the spirit of things. To be in Faith is to think about the spirit of things, to mentally dwell within the spirit of things, to feel the spirit of things and to be filled through and through with the unbounded power of this spirit. Faith never pays any attention to appearances; Faith has information from a higher source; Faith knows that all things are possible now, because to be in Faith is to be in that power that can do all things now. When we try to enter Faith we must give full right-of-way to this power; we must permit this power to thrill every atom in being, and we must give this power the privilege to do whatever we now may desire to have done. The more we depend upon this power the more of this power we shall receive, until our capacity becomes enormous.

To obtain more of the spirit of love, to acquire power from the Infinite Source, to grow in knowledge and wisdom and overcome the defects of our nature, we must have a mind that ever aspires to the highest and best. As a part of the Infinite Mind, we should reach up and demand what we most need. We will have power to obtain results in proportion to the force and earnestness of our thought and desire. Persistent earnest desire is a magnetic power which, when encouraged by Faith and strengthened by effort, will invariably draw to you the thing wished for. Every obstacle that is conquered, every new victory gained, will give you more Faith in your power, and you will have greater ability to win.

When you wish good to materialize, you must have a positive, constructive Faith. Then you are in a position to strengthen and develop it. Perhaps your Faith is only the residue from the background of your childhood; maybe it is a little shriveled from lack of use or tattered and worn from misuse. You still have it, however. All it needs is your awareness of its power, your recognition that you already have it in your possession and the opportunity to express itself in action.

To work with God-power (Consciousness) you must give it right of way and still the reasoning mind. The instant you ask, Infinite Intelligence knows the way of fulfillment. Man's part is to rejoice and give thanks, and act his Faith. A very well known woman in England told of this experience: She was asking, with great feeling, for a realization of God (consciousness). These words came to her "Act as though I were, and I am." It is exactly what I say, over and over again – only active Faith impresses the subconscious, and unless you impress the subconscious, there are no results.

Why did the Nazarene tell us that we must become as little children before we could enter the kingdom of Heaven? Simply because the Faith of a little child is perfect. Everything you tell a child is accepted at its face value, for children have no adverse experience and fears to counteract their Faith.

"O thou of little Faith, wherefore didst thou doubt." Because the power of the Universal Mind is invisible is no reason to doubt it. All the generating powers of existence are invisible; we cannot see Life except as a motive power; love is invisible, yet no one doubts love; and we only see the effects of happiness, peace and health. The same Law that works for us is the Law that Christ used and gave to His disciples. It is just as available to us today as it was when God (consciousness) said, "Let there be Light." The Universal Supply is all around us, and it forms in us and about us according to our thoughts.

Faith is this practical, literal seeing God (consciousness), Life, Spirit, Substance, right here and now. All must come to this knowledge, from the least to the greatest, in one way or another. If not through conscious aspiration (desire, prayer), then through experience, through "hard lines." "Know the Lord: for all shall know me, from the least to the greatest." According to the degree of your acceptance and use of this Presence, which is active Faith, it is established unto you. If you know God (consciousness) as Life and Harmony, you have Health, you are Health. If you know God (consciousness) as Abundance, you lack no good thing. It depends upon your Faith.

You have the right to ask your Father because he is your Father. If you know your right to ask and stand at the door and demand principle to work for you, it must respond to the call of your consciousness and fulfill your need. Such is the value of this wonderful impersonal law, open for the use of all. The great point to be borne in mind is that Faith is a law, and being such, must produce for those who use it. In your garden there may be a tree laden with ripe apples. A good man, so called, may shake the tree. He will get apples. A bad man, so called, may shake the tree. He will get apples. Getting the apples is not the result of being either good or bad, but in having the knowledge to shake the tree, or do that which releases the fruit. Even so, fulfilling the law of Faith produces the demonstration, for demonstration is the result of applied principle. When you discover that God (consciousness), in giving you dominion in earth, gave you a law through which to exercise your dominion, you will rejoice because of the freedom that lies before you in your opportunity of bringing freedom to others. Faith worketh in love, and the magical, wonder-working power of this law will make you love God (consciousness), the giver of it, in a way you have never known to love him before.

Faith gives one a sublime assurance of one's good. One may be surrounded by adverse appearances, but this sublime assurance impresses the subconscious mind, and a way open for the manifestation of health, wealth and happiness. There is an endless, invisible supply for every man. "Before we called we are answered." This supply is waiting to be released by Faith and the spoken word.

Moreover, in all of the esoteric teaching and doctrine, so announced by the founders of the great religions and their successors, you will find that the Road to the Recognition, Realization and Manifestation of the Truth is always that of the Path of Faith. Even before Works, there is placed Faith. Before the manifestation, there must come the full realization; and before the full realization must come the full recognition and the perception, accompanied by the deep feeling of Faith. Before the believer may justly expect to reap, he must sow the seeds of Confident Expectation. Everywhere we find the repeated and constantly reiterated note of Faith, Faith, Faith! We are constantly admonished to have Faith, coupled with the promise that if Faith be had and maintained "all the rest shall be added unto you."

We are now coming into an understanding age. We no longer have the Faith of peasants, we have understanding Faith. Solomon said: "With all your getting, get understanding"; understanding of the working of Spiritual Law, so that we distribute this power within us in a constructive way. The law of laws, is to do unto others as you would be done by; for, whatever you send out comes back and what you do to others will be done to you. So, the woman who refrains from criticizing, saves herself from criticism. Critical people are always being criticized. They are living in that vibration.

Faith is a part of the soul; it is inseparably united with the soul; one can never lose all his Faith, but one can increase its power without end; and as the power of Faith is increased, by having more Faith, the expression of life will increase, and everything that comes from life will increase.

By hard and persistent work, concentrating all the energies of body and mind in the effort to achieve the thing desired, being thorough and honest, enthusiastic and kind, having Faith in one's natural ability and innate power, there is no task too difficult and no environment so fraught with obstacles which one may not conquer. When every faculty of the mind, every nerve center of the body, every muscle and every cell become completely polarized to the spark of life which glows within the invisible center of the higher self, then every word will be a sovereign decree and every act a perfect manifestation of the word. As long as you remain ignorant of the fact that life is omnipresent and that you are an inseparable part of that life, you will fail to appropriate that which is rightfully yours, and will live and move in a circle that is limited by your own thoughts and acts.

"**According to your Faith be it unto you.**" Faith is expectancy, "According to your Faith, be it unto you." We might say, according to your expectancies be it done unto you; so, what are you expecting? We hear people say: "We expect the worst to happen," or "The worst is yet to come." They are deliberately inviting the worst to come. We hear others say: "I expect a change for the better." They are inviting better conditions into their lives. Change your expectancies and you change your conditions. How can you change your expectancies, when you have formed the habit of expecting loss, lack or failure? Begin to act as if you expected success, happiness and abundance; prepare for your good. Do something to show you expect it to come. Active Faith alone, will impress the subconscious.

Fear, which is Faith in negative, is an agent of doubt and often the cause of it. It is Faith misdirected. It is Faith in evil. God (consciousness) didn't plant failure, limitation, trouble, worry, fear and disease in you. You thought them up yourself, fed them with your thought and attention, kept them alive with your belief and so continued to attract them to your experience.

Faith is a magnetic power that attracts the answer to your prayer. Results do not come by chance, accident, or fate. They are molded by your Faith in your power through God (consciousness).

Faith is the first of the cardinal virtues. To it we are to add power, and to that power, understanding, and to that, self-control. Faith is the bedrock principle when we start to build a well body, a calm, strong mentality, or a conquering spirit. Faith is just intelligent confidence in something or somebody. It is invincible in connection with action. Without works it is dead. It must believe the God (consciousness) of health, and then do the things that make for health. In this way it faces the impossible and cries, it shall be done, and it is. There are no limitations. All things are possible to this combination. We usually do what we believe we can do. We get what we believe we shall get. We become what we believe we shall become. Cultivate your Faith by getting it into action. Believe and keep right on believing and doing, and all things are yours.

Faith must be used by you for yourself if you desire freedom. It is your Faith that saves you . . not the Faith of another. Therefore, grow large in your conception of the power of Faith, and in the realization of your responsibility and privilege in applying it. Since it is God's (consciousness's) gift, you displease him if you do not use it. The Father does not desire to see you in limitation or lack of any kind. "He satisfieth the desire of every living creature." His great longing is that you shall recognize him as the one who satisfies, or fulfills, the desire. All seeming lack is but an invitation urging you to the acceptance of God (consciousness) as the fulfillment of it.

Faith knows that the obstacle we think we see is an illusion; it does not exist in reality; it is only a belief produced by our inability to reach any further than we do; but Faith dispels this belief; Faith leads consciousness on in every direction, and proves to mind that we may go as far as we like anywhere, we shall find substantial footing everywhere, without a single obstacle in the way. Faith knows that there is something everywhere; and to him who has Faith this something is revealed.

With the consciousness of power, the love for high attainment and the unwavering resolve, there must also be Faith in the harmony and goodness of the laws and forces you invoke to your aid. If you remain true to the highest monitions, and are not led astray by the counter influences which constantly appear, if your love for the attainment of the highest and best is greater than your attraction toward all that is unworthy, you will bring to your aid the host of invisible powers which work on the human plane for the upliftment of man. In countless ways you will have unmistakable evidence of help from unseen sources, which will strengthen your Faith in the divine leadings and give courage to reach up and attain. Let your watchword be onward, and turn not back; but with your eyes fixed on the final goal, with uplifted, eager hands, continue to tread the path which leads towards the heights; and know that the time will come when that mysterious force within you, which now causes the heart to beat with infinite longings, will not be silenced until you have received response to every yearning and realized the fulfillment of every hope.

Although the subconscious Faithfully serves man, it must not be inferred that the relation is that of a servant to a master as was anciently conceived. The ancient prophets called it the slave and servant of man. St. Paul personified it as a "woman" and said: "The woman should be subject to man in everything" The subconscious does serve man and Faithfully gives form to his feelings. However, the subconscious has a distinct distaste for compulsion and responds to persuasion rather than to command; consequently, it resembles the beloved wife more than the servant. "The husband is head of the wife," may not be true of man and woman in their earthly relationship, but it is true of the conscious and the subconscious, or the male and female aspects of consciousness. The mystery to which Paul referred when he wrote, "This is a great mystery... He that loveth his wife loveth himself... And they two shall be one flesh", is simply the mystery of consciousness. Consciousness is really one and undivided but for creation's sake it appears to be divided into two.

To increase the potential of Faith, you must increase your expectations. To become skillful in Faith, you must practice Faith.

Faith is the bridge between the physical and Spiritual world. You have the privilege of crossing on it at will.

The LOA is a new way of thinking. This new way of thinking has to BE a habit . . the old way of thinking has to be discarded. I AM . . not I WILL . . We have to BE before we can have. We have to BE (within) before we can have our desire manifest. Saying I WILL, will keep it from manifesting. Saying I AM going to, will keep it from manifesting. Observe your inner talking . . for out of our inner talking are the issues of our life. I AM is the power that does all. And I AM That . . I AM

Faith is a mental attitude against which there is no possibility of contradiction. If that attitude is directed toward God (consciousness), it becomes your ability to do anything.

Know that any desire you hold in Faith is a Reality in Spirit, existing from the moment you conceived it and eagerly awaiting its manifestation in your life. Put your Faith to the test. Exercise it. Let it grow.

The things you hold most in thought and imagination you will make a reality. But there must be steadfastness of purpose and persistent Faith and effort. To say to yourself daily, "I can and I will," to send an unbroken current of thought in the direction of the desire, to aim well and to neglect nothing that will aid you, will insure the final realization of every reasonable ambition. But if you have courage today and make spasmodic efforts, and the next day feel depressed and are doubtful, you will send out destructive forces which will hinder your progress. Negative, despondent, irritable thoughts are as potent to destroy as are positive, hopeful, courageous thoughts to build up. If your mind wanders, if you doubt and hesitate, if you lack Faith and persistency of purpose, you will continue to drift with the tide of circumstances discouraged and helpless on life's surging sea. The great starting point to freedom and power is the conservation of force. Force is omnipresent. The most important problem is not how to get force, but how to conserve, arouse and wisely direct the force already at command. The physical organism is like an engine, and the mind is the engineer. If the boiler is full of holes, the force will be dissipated, and the machine cannot do effective work. You must stop the leakage, the useless waste by dissipation, and the worry and discontent arising from a distorted imagination. You must cultivate more constructive thought and put vital force into all your actions. You must learn to concentrate the mind to the consideration of a single thing, at any given time, to the exclusion of all else. And everything you do should be a stepping stone to some fruitful end. The mind must become steadfast and unwavering, and your thoughts creative, expressing the highest and best within. Only as you have health and happiness and use the force of body and faculties of mind aright can you rise to the threshold of the perfect way.

"For verily I say unto you, if ye have Faith as a grain of mustard seed, ye shall say unto this mountain, remove hence to yonder place; and it shall remove; and nothing shall be impossible unto you."

This Faith of a grain of mustard seed has proved a stumbling block to man. He has been taught to believe that a grain of mustard seed signifies a small degree of Faith. So he naturally wonders why he, a mature man, should lack this insignificant measure of Faith when so small an amount assures success.

A mustard seed is conscious of being a mustard seed and a mustard seed alone. It is not aware of any other seed in the world. It is sealed in the conviction that it is a mustard seed in the same manner that the spermatozoa sealed in the womb is conscious of being man and only man.

A grain of mustard seed is truly the measure of Faith necessary to accomplish your every objective; but like the mustard seed you too must lose yourself in the consciousness of being only the thing desired. You abide within this sealed state until it bursts itself and reveals your conscious claim.

Perhaps the Faith you have now is just enough Faith to let you try Faith. Tend the seed with Love and confidence. Water it with persistency and tenacity. Shelter, the tiny growth from the cold winds of negative thought.

Make a mental picture of your desire as Fulfilled now, and now only, making the mental picture complete, vivid, alive with feeling. This is the meaning of the statement to "Ask believing that you (already) have." In the mental picture you actually do have (mentally, which is the realm of all true causation) your desire right now. Once you really get into the Feeling that what you want already is yours (mentally) you will soon realize how quickly it grows into actual form. Keep out of your mind all fear-habits of thought. Know that fear-habits can be readily changed into Faith-habits. Fear and Faith are the same, one being one end of the stick and the other the other end of the same stick. The fear-end of the stick is a shovel and will surely dig the grave of success; the FAITH-end is a Jeweled Crown ready to adorn the head of any who will wear it.

People are beginning to realize the power of their words and thoughts. They understand why "Faith is the substance of the thing hoped for, the evidence of things not seen." We see the law of expectancy working out through superstition. If you walk under a ladder and expect it to give you bad luck, it will give you bad luck. The ladder is quite innocent; bad luck came because you expected it. We might say, expectancy is the substance of the things hoped for; or expectancy is the substance of the thing man fears; "The thing I expected has come upon me."

Speak those things that you desire to happen as if they already have and persist in this feeling (Faith) and they will become a part of your experience. But heed the spiritual law of secrecy. You are not trying to convince others of the truth of your statements, you are dropping a seed into your subconscious to be brought to fruition through the law. Faith in your own words are the watering of the seed.

We speak of enlarging our Faith, but the only way in which we can do this is by enlarging our mental equivalents, by increasing our demands and by adding the quality of gratitude. When we believe that God (consciousness) wants through us the thing we want, we are ready to give thanks in advance.

If you say and believe, "I have Faith in the substance of God (consciousness) working in and through me to increase and bring abundance into my world," your Faith will start to work mightily in the mind substance and make you prosperous. Whatever you put into substance along with Faith will work out in manifestation in your world.

To practice concentration and gain control over the creative force of thought, will enable one who has perseverance and Faith to push steadily forward to broader fields of usefulness. If you desire to make the best possible use of your natural talents, to control great interests, to become the leader of great movements which will help the world to advance to a more ideal state of existence, hold your mind in meditation upon the power desired, until every obstacle in the way of its attainment has been removed. By Faith, perseverance and concentrated effort, fixing the attention unwaveringly upon the thing that is to be accomplished, you will arouse an element of power which will invariably produce results. You should have some high purpose, some noble ideal, to which everything else in life is subordinated. If you have no definite aim upon which to concentrate your energies, your life will be a failure. A person with an ordinary mind, by concentrating his forces on one supreme aim, will accomplish more than the most talented and gifted who dissipate their energies by sending their thoughts in too many directions.

Man's supply is inexhaustible and unfailing when fully trusted, but Faith or trust must precede the demonstration. "According to your Faith be it unto you." "Faith is the substance of things hoped for, the evidence of things not see . . "for Faith holds the vision steady, and the adverse pictures are dissolved and dissipated, and "in due season we shall reap, if we faint not."

Paul tells us that: "Faith is the substance of a thing hoped for, the evidence of a thing unseen." Give that a moment's thought . . Faith is the substance, the actual substance of anything we desire. The reason we have not demonstrated more Faith is because of our lack of understanding. We have not understood that everything works in exact accord with a definite law. We must build our desires in our world within, build them in Faith, hope, courage, and hold them regardless of outside appearance. Pay no attention to appearance. Your success, your happiness and your health are all of your own making, and if you are not satisfied with conditions as they are you have only to visualize them as you would have them to be in order to change them. The Law will work for you every time when you are working with the Law and for the good of all concerned.

In Jewish and Christian theology, Faith is "that mental act of man which places him in an acceptable relation to God (consciousness)." In Mohammedanism, Faith in Allah is a prerequisite to knowledge of the Divine, and the bestowal of Divine aid. In Hinduism, Faith in Brahman is the Master Key. In Buddhism, Faith in "The Law which makes for Good" is an absolute necessity to the seeker after Nirvana. Everywhere, Faith is held to be the first, and absolutely necessary step toward Attainment. If this be true concerning the exoteric teaching and doctrine, it is thrice true of the esoteric presentation of the Truth . . for in the latter it takes on a mystic and occult significance. As an ancient mystic once said: "There is a White Magic in Faith which transcends all other forms or powers of Magic."

Do not fear. Have Faith. Though the shadows of sorrow and adversity gather about you, do not fear. You are a child of the Infinite. The Divine Light within will cause the darkness to flee and the phantoms to vanish. Have courage. There is a power within you which will make you the master over every circumstance and condition. Invoke the aid of the higher potencies. Let the heart be brave, the hand steady and the will unwavering. Have Faith in your power to attain all that is good, all that is true and desirable. Breathe inspiration and life into all effort. Be persistent, hopeful and patient. It is within your power to gratify the cherished ambition which lies nearest your heart, be it the desire for wealth, love or fame, for health and happiness or high attainment in any field of human endeavor. The power to realize your ideals is within yourself, so also are the barriers which stand in the way of present manifestation. The greatest enemies to progress are fear and doubt, weakness and ignorance, and belief in limitations. To come into an understanding of the omnipotence of thought will give you the assurance and strength to accomplish seemingly impossible results. You will have Faith in your power to overcome difficulties. You will assume responsibilities and command a force and inspiration which will insure the success of your ventures.

The highest Faith is whole, continuous, triumphant, and victorious. It admits no contrary evidence, no fear, no opposition, no separation, and no limitation.

The lavish assumption that Faith is so paramount a quality that its possession is alone sufficient to secure the salvation of the believer needs to be corrected by examination of the forms under which it has been manifested in the past. Only in that way can we appreciate the extent to which Faith has proved itself an untrustworthy guide to life, not only in assuming knowledge which it did not possess, but in carrying that imaginary knowledge into action prejudicial welfare.

If you have any great undertaking to accomplish which will benefit the world as well as yourself, you will receive help and encouragement from countless invisible sources. If your heart is right, your desires noble, your aims lofty, you will receive help in many mysterious ways which will strengthen your Faith in the Divine leading. As you seek earnestly to cooperate with the evolutionary forces of nature you will unite yourself with all the enkindling sympathies of life. Your ideals will expand, your Faith will grow stronger and you will reach up into the realm of cause and attract all power needed to manifest the harmonies of that larger and broader and more sympathetic life which recognizes man's vital relationship to the Infinite.

Hope says that it could happen or it might happen. Faith says that it will happen. Faith is the moving force in all creative processes.

Your Faith simply acts to reveal that which already is. The works come automatically to the heart that believes.

Faith not only leads man into a definite course of action but opens the way for the Power to flow along the uncongested circuits of his thought.

Instead of trying to set the world right, set the ideals of your own life right. Work out every problem from within. All growth is from within. The way to change things is to change in consciousness first of all. May heaven pity the rest of the world if we, who know the truth, are living anything else than the ideal today. If we, who know the truth of life, find it necessary to turn to outside agencies to make things right, what shall the struggling multitudes do? Dare to fling yourself on the bosom of the Law. Dare to say, "It shall be done unto me." Dare to believe that you can better get results through Faith than through struggle. Stop struggling! Struggle raises resistance, and resistance brings upon you the very evil you deplore.

One of the greatest messages given to the race through the scriptures is that God (consciousness) is man's supply and that man can release, through his spoken word, all that belongs to him by divine right. He must, however, have perfect Faith in his spoken word. Isaiah said, "My word shall not return unto me void, but shall accomplish that where unto it is sent." We know now, that words and thoughts are a tremendous vibratory force, ever molding man's body and affairs.

By conserving the energies which are being constantly generated and transmuted, and being governed at all times by the law of use in the expenditure of force on the physical and mental planes, directing the finest and most subtle elements thus generated toward the realization of the things wished for, you will become a living magnet to draw from the material world all that is desirable. Realize that nothing is greater, nothing more powerful than a well defined thought, or image, set up in your mind, clothed with the magnetic elements of your being and sent out and sustained by an unwavering Faith in the fulfillment of its mission.

When you believe that your desire is already fulfilled, believe that what you are asking for is already yours, you have put your Faith to work and what you seek will be manifested in your experience.

To keep the mind in the right current of thought will endow the body with more strength, more power of endurance and give it more symmetry and beauty. To keep the mind in the right state to attract more and more of the Supreme Force will give ability to realize every desire and demand. When you demand power from the unseen you may rest assured that you will receive the force needed to accomplish your plan or purpose. The Supreme Power is always at the command of one who places his mind in a childlike attitude to receive. To have Faith in the existence of that power as you have Faith in the law of gravitation, to cooperate with it and direct it, will give you unlimited capacity. The one who is most successful in life keeps his mind in the attitude of cooperation with the Supreme Power. To keep in touch with the unseen currents of power will give inspiration, courage and insight. You will have Faith in the goodness of law. You will know that every earnest demand will obtain an answer. Every desire of your heart will be gratified. In thought you will never acknowledge an impossibility.

All that I have is thine. Are you a beggar sitting on a bag of gold? Are you slumbering on the brink of the Infinite power? Behold! You stand this day at the entrance to a land of tremendous possibilities. Son, thou art ever with me, and all that I have is thine. This all is yours if you have the Faith to accept it, if you believe that you already have it, if you let it manifest AS YOU.

Faith and expectancy impress the subconscious mind with the picture of fulfillment. In the 23rd Psalm we read, "He restoreth my soul." Your soul is your subconscious mind and must be restored with the right ideas. Whatever you feel deeply is impressed upon the subconscious, and manifests in your affairs. If you are convinced that you are a failure, you will be a failure, until you impress the subconscious with the conviction you are a success.

There are many who have learned to invoke the aid of the Infinite Power. They have Faith in themselves because they are sustained by immortal energies. It does not matter to them if things seem uncertain. They may not be able to see the pathway of their future. But they know that it will lead them upward to greater joy, to wider freedom. They know that the eternal and constant law of progress will lead them on. They know they will emerge from the shadow, from every sorrow. They know that the Infinite Light is shining steadfastly in the heavens, and they will be led by its beckoning ray. You need to have more Faith in yourself, Faith in the laws of life, Faith in the Infinite Power of which your being is an inseparable part. Why lack Faith when you see the evidence of truth and justice, of wisdom and love in every star, in the order and beauty of nature, in the golden glow of the sunset?

We will say that you have some desire or wish you want fulfilled, or that you need some special advice. You first clearly picture what is wanted and then you concentrate on getting it. Have absolute Faith that your desires will be realized. Believe that it will according to your belief be fulfilled. Never, at this time, attempt to analyze the belief. You don't care anything about the whys and wherefores. You want to gain the thing you desire, and if you concentrate on it in the right way you will get it. A Caution. Never think you will not succeed, but picture what is wanted as already yours, and yours it surely will be.

All visible things are the result of invisible causes. Your present environment is an expression of past thoughts and desires. To have a beautiful environment, your thoughts which create it must be harmonious. The real elements of success are in the mind. When there is clearness of perception, harmony of thought, force and determination, there will come a corresponding expression in the, outer world. Fill the mind with brightness, banish gloom and despondency, have Faith in the Supreme Power, and work incessantly to demonstrate the law that whatever we earnestly and persistently desire shall be obtained.

The measure of man's success in any direction is determined by the predominant state of his mind. If you are hopeful, enthusiastic and courageous, and do not yield to the influence of despondency and doubt, you are sending out forces which will attract the good; and as your Faith becomes stronger in your ability to control and direct your thoughts, you will absorb the finer elements which bring health, peace, happiness and all things desired. It is difficult to keep permanently in a hopeful, confident mood of mind, as there are times when progress is slow and the opposing influences seem greater than the forces which aid. But the man who has Faith in his power, the man who sees only the good and knows that from every experience will come more strength and greater persistency, wisdom and courage, will bend all things to his purpose and make every circumstance aid him in material advancement. Having a definite aim always in view, a thought force is generated which is felt by all with whom you have dealings.

Conscious of himself as at one with the Creative Intelligence, he must then seek how he may reproduce Its activity in the control of his own conditions and affairs. He must awaken to his powers. He must learn to use the creative word. He must put forth his thought that it may embody itself in fitting form. He must know that he needs but "to speak the word only and my servant shall be healed." His word is the image or picture of his desire. The more Faith he has in it, the better the results; but no word lacks power. Creative Mind begins to act on every word that is spoken.

Faith is feeling or living in the consciousness of being the thing desired; Faith is the secret of creation. By Faith God (your consciousness) calleth things that are not seen as though they were and makes them seen. It is Faith which enables you to become conscious of being the thing desired; again, it is Faith which seals you in this conscious state until your invisible claim ripens to maturity and expresses itself, is made visible. Faith or feeling is the secret of this appropriation. Through feeling, the consciousness desiring is joined to the thing desired. How would you feel if you were that which you desire to be? Wear the mood, this feeling that would be yours if you were already that which you desire to be; and in a little while you will be sealed in the belief that you are. Then without effort this invisible state will objectify itself; the invisible will be made visible.

What a light would come into our lives, what invincible power would come into our Minds, what a cleansing of the soul and body would result if we made use of this inner force of Faith! New wine, Jesus called it . . wine that bursts old wine skins of limited patterns and demands a new Consciousness to hold it. We don't need new Faith or more Faith to be transformed. We need only to renew our Faith in the Faith we already have.

The things which the mind dwells on the most become a reality. If your mind dwells on the dark side of things you will attract all that is morbid and unnatural. If you entertain negative thoughts, if you lack Faith in your power to do a thing, you will fail in every effort. You are making environments for yourself in the future by the thoughts you are holding most in mind. If you are living now in imagination in better surroundings, if you are sending out the silent demand for improved conditions, for greater attainments, you are creating forces which will draw to you the better things. To aspire to make the best use of your talents will give an ever increasing capacity for attainment. As you approach nearer to the Infinite Mind, you will have more Faith in yourself and will receive fresh inspiration and courage. When you put your dependence and trust in the Supreme Power you will attract the idea, the event, the opportunity for realizing the thing you desire.

Faith is alive and it leads to more life. Doubt is dead and leads nowhere. The leading characteristic of Faith is that it constantly flows and burns with constantly increasing brightness and expectancy. Faith always travels in the one direction of understanding. Doubt is a blight upon every effort towards Truth.

We do not see the Law of Faith, but we know its power by what it does.

According to your Faith . . your Faith in God (consciousness), your Faith in yourself, your Faith in your goal, your Faith in your ability, you get results. The man of little Faith gets small results; the man of big Faith gets large results. According to your Faith be it unto you. We can never go beyond the realization of our mental equivalents.

We must grow into a Faith in the existence of the Supreme Force and our ability to draw to us an unlimited supply for every purpose and demand. It will come to us and give an increase of strength and inspiration in all effort, all progress, as we learn to keep the mind in the right attitude of Faith in the reality of this power and maintain the earnest desire to receive it. Attracting force from the unseen makes all work a pleasure. We feel our nearness to the source of all things, and know that nothing can take from us its help and protection.

So prepare for your "unforeseen good." Let every thought and every act express your unwavering Faith. Every event in your life is a crystallized idea. Something you have invited through either fear or Faith. Something you have prepared for. So let us be wise and bring oil for our lamps . . and when we least expect it, we shall reap the fruits of our Faith. My lamps are now filled with the oil of Faith and fulfillment.

Faith not only makes old things new, but it is the point of contact between God (consciousness) and man.

It is only by steady, persistent holding of right thought that error can be displaced. If you are not at once very successful in your work (so far as appearances go) remember Faith develops as a grain of mustard seed unfolds. Do not say or allow yourself to believe that you can do nothing because as yet you can do but little. Small Faith is living Faith and holds within itself the seed of gigantic Faith . . Faith so great and so potential that it can remove obstacles comparable to great mountains.

Success reduced to its lowest and simplest terms is Faith expressed in action.

Faith is the belief that you have the power to do all things.

No man is equipped for any undertaking in life unless he has Faith . . the real, living Faith; the Faith that does things; the Faith that can make all things possible.

Your Faith Is Your Fortune: Your Unlimited Power

There is no possible source for anything outside of the Infinite Power, for it embraces everything that is. There is no center or place which confines it, yet it is not absent from the minutest point in space. No object or idea can have existence apart from it, for it is omnipresent. It is the only reality of life. It is impossible for the human mind to fathom the mystery of this power, which had no beginning and can have no ending. The more we apprehend of its workings the more evidence we have that its manifestation is governed by immutable laws. Every individuality composing mankind is an inseparable part of this power. The recognition and Faith in its reality will enable you to appropriate intelligently and draw upon it as much as you will for your happiness and success. It is a never failing force which you may learn to use in all efforts. It will manifest through you in greater fullness as you keep your mind in the right current of thought. You must cease trying to generate force by a spasmodic effort. Call your wandering thoughts to a peaceful center within the mind, place your reliance on the Supreme Power which you feel flowing to you from the unseen, and use your will only to direct that power as it plays through you, as you would steer a boat that is moved by the wind. To you as a part of the Supreme Power belong knowledge and wisdom and all things you can receive and appropriate. You will gain increasing power to draw from the exhaustless source in proportion to the force of demand. Keep in mind the idea that you are a magnet drawing from the universe all things necessary for happiness. You are made of forces which you have drawn to yourself by repeated demands. These forces have been built into your body, and have become literally a part of your flesh and blood. If you have entertained negative, timid, despondent thoughts, you have a corresponding weak, disordered body. If you have earnestly demanded of the Infinite the things which will elevate and ennoble and give strength and courage, these principles are incorporated and will act on you for perfect wholeness, beauty and refinement.

Your Faith Is Your Fortune: Your Unlimited Power

Suggested Reading

Robert Collier - "The Secret of the Ages"

Robert Collier - "The Secret of Gold"

Napoleon Hill - "Think and Grow Rich"

Annie Rix Militz - Prosperity Through the Knowledge and Power of Mind

Joseph Murphy - Your Infinite Power to Be Rich

Anthony Norvell - Money Magnetism - How to Grow Rich Beyond Your Wildest Dreams

Franklyn Hobbs - The Secret of Wealth

Benjamin Franklin - The Way to Wealth

Julia Seton Sears M.D. - The Key to Health, Wealth and Love

Charles Fillmore - Prosperity

John Seaman Garns - Prosperity Plus

Franklin Fillmore Farrington - Realizing Prosperity

Florence Barnard - The Prosperity Book

James Allen - Eight Pillars of Prosperity

Bernard C. Ruggles - Creative Abundance; The Psychology of Ability and Plenty

Metaphysical / Law of Attraction Books

David Allen - The Power of I AM (2014), The Power of I AM - Volume 2 (2015), The Power of I AM - Volume 3 (2017)

David Allen - The Creative Power of Thought, Man's Greatest Discovery (2017)

David Allen - The Secrets, Mysteries & Powers of The Subconscious Mind (2017)

David Allen - The Money Bible - The Secrets of Attracting Prosperity (2017)

David Allen - Your Faith Is Your Fortune, Your Unlimited Power

The Neville Goddard Collection (All 10 of his books plus 2 Lecture series) (2016)

Neville Goddard - Assumptions Harden Into Facts: The Book (2016)

Neville Goddard - Imagination: The Redemptive Power in Man (2016)

Neville Goddard - The World is At Your Command - The Very Best of Neville Goddard (2017)

Neville Goddard - Imagining Creates Reality - 365 Mystical Daily Quotes (2017)

Neville Goddard's Interpretation of Scripture (2018)

The Definitive Christian D. Larson Collection (6 Volumes, 30 books) (2014)

NOTES

NOTES

www.ingramcontent.com/pod-product-compliance
Lightning Source LLC
Chambersburg PA
CBHW020423010526
44118CB00010B/389